The Low-Carb Bible

pi

Publications International, Ltd.

Contributing Writer: Elizabeth M. Ward, M.S., R.D., is a registered dietitian, freelance writer, and nutrition consultant who has worked as a nutrition counselor at Harvard Vanguard Medical Associates. She is the author of *Pregnancy Nutrition: Good Health for You and Your Baby* and coauthor of *Live Longer & Better: A Lifestyle Guide with Recipes and Much More.* Her articles have appeared in the *Los Angeles Times, The Boston Globe, Environmental Nutrition, Fitness, American Baby,* and *Shape Fit Pregnancy,* and she frequently appears on local and national television.

Consultant: Barbara Quinn, M.S., R.D., is a registered dietitian and certified diabetes educator (CDE). She is a pediatric obesity specialist with the University of California, San Francisco. Quinn writes "On Nutrition," a weekly column for the *Monterey County Herald* that is distributed by McClatchy Tribune News Service. She works in the Diabetes and Nutrition Therapy Program at Community Hospital of the Monterey Peninsula.

Nutritional Analysis: Linda R. Yoakam, M.S., R.D., L.D.

Every effort has been made to check the accuracy of the nutritional information that appears with each recipe. However, because numerous variables account for a wide range of values for certain foods, nutritive analyses in this book should be considered approximate.

All recipes and recipe photographs copyright © Publications International, Ltd.

Royalty-Free Photo Credits:
Corbis RF, Getty, PIL Collection, Shutterstock, Stockbyte, Superstock, Deborah Van Kirk

Pictured on the front cover *(top to bottom):* Chocolate Peanut Butter Ice Cream Sandwiches *(page 234)* and Sirloin with Sweet Carmelized Onions *(page 154).*

Pictured on the back cover *(top to bottom):* Grilled Red Snapper with Avocado-Papaya Sauce *(page 132),* Stir-Fried Asparagus *(page 200)* and Strawberry-Topped Cheesecake Cups *(page 236).*

Cover and title page illustration by Shutterstock

contents

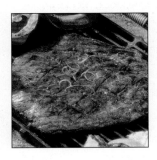

5   get the lowdown on low carb

6   know your low-carb options

    8   low-carb fundamentals

   13   what the research says

   18   are low-carb diets for everyone?

   20   diet reviews

     20   the carbohydrate addict's diet

     22   the new atkins for a new you

     24   the new sugar busters!

     26   the paleo diet

     28   the protein power lifeplan

     30   the schwarzbein principle II

     32   the south beach diet supercharged

     34   suzanne somers' sexy forever

     36   the zone

     38   diets at a glance

40 personalize your low-carb plan

42 how to build your own low-carb diet
50 exercise: the universal fitness tool
56 walk off pounds!
62 strengthening exercises to burn more fat
68 get to know the glycemic index
70 pay attention to portion size
72 measure your success
74 the nutrient counter

104 enjoy low-carb recipes

106 great-start breakfasts
120 satisfying main dishes
186 sensational side dishes
206 super snacks
234 dazzling desserts

249 recipe index

254 general index

get the lowdown on low carb

You want to go low carb, but you want to do it right. You want to lose weight without harming your health, you want a diet that will fit your personality, your tastes, and your life, and you want your weight loss to last.

That's not too much to ask, is it? Not when you have *The Low-Carb Bible* at hand. It's designed to help you create a low-carb lifestyle that will fulfill all these needs.

The Low-Carb Bible guides you from the very start of your low-carb weight-loss quest. And it's there as you progress, to help you make smart, safe choices and get the most from your weight-loss efforts.

The first section of the book, Know Your Low-Carb Options, explains the fundamentals of low-carb dieting, discusses the science that supports its usefulness, and provides warnings about conditions that make low-carb dieting less than desirable. It also includes reviews of popular low-carb plans. The review for each diet describes the reasoning behind its approach to weight loss, the kinds and amounts of foods allowed, how flexible it is, how it might impact your health, and more.

Then, in the second section, Personalize Your Low-Carb Plan, you'll find tools to help you create or tailor a low-carb plan to ensure you get the nutrients your body needs without all the processed foods and empty carbs that do little for your body but pack on pounds. You'll find expert advice on building a low-carb lifestyle that includes plenty of enjoyable physical activity, provides a huge variety of tasty food choices, and works in the real world.

Finally, in the last section, Enjoy Low-Carb Recipes, you'll be amazed to discover the many scrumptious dishes, including desserts, that can be a part of your low-carb plan. The accompanying nutritional information makes it easy for you to plan meals that meet your needs for weight loss, health, and eating pleasure.

You can make low-carb dieting work for you. You just need to know how to take the greatest advantage of its weight-loss potential while preserving your health and preventing the boredom that has sunk many a diet in the past. In other words, you just need to keep *The Low-Carb Bible* nearby. So enjoy weight loss for a change!

know your low-carb options

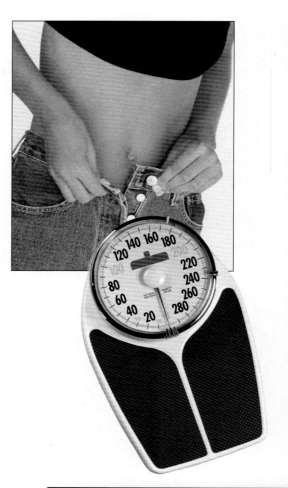

With all the low-carb diets out there, how do you know which one's right for you? After all, just because a diet worked for a friend or celebrity doesn't mean it will work for you. To help you decide, this section provides you with an understanding of the basics of low-carb dieting, what the research says about it, and what warnings you need to be aware of. You'll also find reviews of popular low-carb diet plans, with information and ratings to help you figure out which one suits you and your lifestyle best.

Nutrition Facts
Serving Size 8 fl oz (240ml)
Servings Per Container 2.5

Amount Per Serving
Calories 50

% Daily Value*

Total Fat 0g   0%
Sodium 110mg   5%
Potassium 30mg   0%
Total Carbohydrate 14g 5%
Sugars 14g   1%
Protein 0g   5%

a significant source of Calories From Fat,
ed Fat, Cholesterol, Dietary Fiber,
Vitamin C, Calcium, Iron.
ly Values are based on a 2,000

Nutrition Fac
Serving Size 1 oz (28g) about 1
Servings Per Container about

low-carb fundamentals

A diet is a diet, right? Not according to low-carbohydrate diet proponents, who say they have a better way to shed weight and to keep it off for good. To grasp the logic driving the low-carb revolution, you need to understand the role that carbohydrate, fat, and protein play in the body and how they are used for energy.

the basic idea

The Zone, The South Beach Diet, and *Sugar Busters* are just a few examples of low-carb diet programs. Although they may differ in their approach and style, all low-carb diets have a single uniting principle: Too much dietary carbohydrate causes weight gain and prevents weight loss. Low-carb diets cut down the amount of carbohydrate you eat rather than cutting calories or fat, the usual targets of weight-loss programs.

Some of the low-carb diet plans eliminate more

carbohydrate than others. Dr. Atkins's diet, for instance, allows only 5 percent of daily calories to come from carbohydrate, while The Zone allows 40 percent. Traditional diet recommendations call for 45 to 65 percent of calories from carbohydrate.

carbohydrate: the culprit?

Why do low-carb proponents finger carbohydrate instead of fat (or protein) as the culprit in weight gain or the inability to lose weight? It has to do with the way the body stores excess energy as fat.

Carbohydrates (sugars and starches) are found in breads, cereals, rice, pasta, and other grains; fruits and vegetables; dairy products; and in processed foods as added sugar. During digestion, carbs are broken down into glucose (the type of carbohydrate cells use for energy) and released into the bloodstream. Glucose is the preferred energy source for most tissues, including the brain, which requires a constant source of fuel for peak function. Your body maintains tight control over blood glucose levels. After you eat carbohydrate, blood glucose levels rise. To deliver glucose (energy) from the blood to body tis-

below par when your diet is consistently low in carbohydrates. Liver stores are also easily depleted if you go without food for 12 to 18 hours, which dieters sometimes do when they fast. The body's muscle tissue can pack in more than three times the amount of glycogen as the liver—about 300 grams—but the muscles' glycogen

sues, the pancreas releases insulin, a hormone, into the bloodstream. Insulin facilitates the transfer of glucose from the blood into your cells. Of the three macronutrients (carbohydrate, protein, and fat), carbohydrate causes the greatest and speediest spike in blood glucose levels and, as a result, the largest release of insulin. This, as you'll see, is an important factor to low-carb diet advocates.

Some of the carbohydrate that is not used to meet immediate energy needs becomes glycogen, which is stored in the liver and the muscles for future use. Insulin also facilitates the processes that allow glycogen to be stored in the liver and muscles. The liver can stockpile between 70 and 90 grams of glycogen. When blood glucose levels fall between meals, the stockpile is raided to keep blood glucose levels within normal range. Liver stores are easily depleted when you're on a low-carb diet since liver glycogen stores are

Carbohydrate confusion

Not all carbs are bad, even to low-carb diet proponents. There are two basic types of carbohydrate: simple and complex. It's very important to distinguish between the two.

Simple sugars include table sugar, honey, molasses, and the high fructose corn syrup found in a variety of processed foods, including salad dressings, crackers, cereal, bread, and soda. Simple carbs are also found naturally in fruit and in dairy products as lactose.

Complex carbohydrates include starch and fiber, and they are found in foods such as grains, corn, and potatoes. Complex carbs provide important nutrients, including vitamins, minerals, fiber, and phytonutrients, which are disease-fighting plant compounds. If you drastically reduce complex carbohydrates from your diet, you will lose out on these crucial nutrients and may jeopardize your health, both short- and long-term.

However good they taste, many foods that contain simple carbohydrates aren't worth much from a nutritional standpoint. Your body receives virtually no nutritional benefit from cakes, cookies, and candy, and little nutrition from white or brown-colored bread, white rice, white pasta, and other overly processed foods. Foods filled with simple carbohydrates can add inches to your waistline and set off food cravings, leading you to consume even more.

So, when low-carb proponents advise you to go easy on carbs, they're primarily talking about simple carbohydrates. You can still eat fiber-filled carbohydrates, such as beans, whole grains, fruits, and vegetables. Fiber is a carbohydrate the body cannot digest so it provides no calories and gives your diet "bulk" to help you feel satisfied longer.

stores can only be used to provide the muscles with energy; they can't be used to fuel the rest of the body.

What happens when the liver and muscles are filled to the brim with glycogen? Extra carbohydrate is converted to fat and stored in your cells. Again, this process is facilitated by insulin. That's why low-carb proponents believe that eating a low-carbohydrate diet will help you lose weight. If you don't provide your body with a lot of carbohydrate, your body won't produce a lot of insulin, so it won't be storing as much fat. The less fat stored in your cells, the thinner you will be. That's the premise.

the ketosis controversy. When you eat a very low-carbohydrate diet every day, glucogen stores in the liver become low. Less glucose is available to fuel your cells, prompting the body to turn to fat stores for energy. The liver converts fat to acidic substances called ketones that can be used for energy. This induces an abnormal metabolic condition called ketosis, which is defined as the presence of high levels of ketones in the blood.

Some low-carb proponents encourage ketosis, seeing it as a sign of successful fat burning. Others do not. It's easy to see why some diet plan authors shy away from ketosis. The rapid fat burning that produces ketosis disturbs the body's chemical balance. What's worse, it may lead to dehydration. In

an effort to restore balance, the body eliminates ketones through the urine, causing increased urination. Ketosis can also cause bad breath.

protein power

Low-carb diets are nearly always high-protein diets, and they may also be high in fat. The reason? Only carbohydrate, fat, and protein provide your body with the calories (energy) it needs to function. When you drastically curb consumption of one of the three energy-producing nutrients—in this case, carbohydrates—your only source of energy is one, or both, of the others—in this case, protein and/or fat.

Life would be impossible without protein, found in foods such as meat, eggs, poultry, seafood, dairy products, and legumes. Protein is necessary for relaying messages in the nervous system and brain; balancing fluid; absorbing nutrients; and producing enzymes, hormones, connective tissue, muscles, antibodies, and other substances that affect growth, development, and overall health. Digestion breaks protein down into its individual amino acids, which can be used to construct body proteins such as insulin, red blood cells, and digestive enzymes, or to make glucose for energy.

Protein does not cause the sharp increase in blood glucose levels that carbohydrate does. Instead, protein produces a slower and steadier increase in blood sugar. As a result, the pancreas releases less insulin— the hormone that helps the body store excess glucose as fat. That is why low-carbohydrate proponents encourage dieters to eat fewer calories from carbohydrates—which stimulate more insulin release—and more calories from protein. If you eat more calories from protein than you need, however, your body will still store the excess as fat.

fat: friend or foe?

Dieters tend to despise fat, but they are misguided. Fat provides the raw materials (fatty acids) for your body's production of many substances that drive life and sustain good health, including brain cells. For instance, fat is required by the body to absorb and transport vitamins A, D, E, and K.

Fatty acids are classified as either saturated or unsaturated (these include

monounsaturated or polyunsaturated). Saturated fats, found in foods including meat, cheese, and cream, contribute to clogged arteries and increase your risk for heart attack and stroke. Unsaturated fats, found in vegetable oils, nuts, avocados, and seafood, are considered good for your heart because they lower the levels of harmful fats, such as cholesterol, in the blood.

Fat's bad reputation, from a weight-loss perspective, comes from the fact that one gram of fat contains nine calories. Compare that with carbohydrate and protein, each of which provide just four calories per gram. Fat, then, supplies more than double the calories of the other two macronutrients. The risk of overindulging in fat-laden foods when you're trying to lose weight is that you'll also be consuming a high-calorie diet, one that will add pounds rather than take them off.

But low-carb proponents have a different angle on fat. The number of calories it provides is only a part of

When insulin goes awry

Obesity and lack of exercise may result in insulin resistance (IR), which affects an estimated 100 million Americans. IR means that the insulin you produce and release into the bloodstream is not effective to move glucose out of the blood and into the cells because cells are "resistant" to the action of insulin. As a result, blood glucose levels rise in spite of high concentrations of insulin. High-carb diets, particularly those packed with simple carbs, may aggravate IR in some people. Since being overweight and underactive are major contributors to its development, IR can often be reversed with weight loss, increased physical activity, or a combination of both.

In search of satisfaction

Eating more protein may be one key to weight control because it promotes feelings of satisfaction in the brain. In fact, a high-protein diet may head off feelings of dietary deprivation that so often prompt dieters to throw in the towel. How much protein is safe to eat on a daily basis? For healthy people, 100 grams or less probably poses no health problems. For comparison: 12 ounces of meat, fish, or poultry provides about 80 grams of protein. Protein is also found in eggs, cheese and nuts and even in carbohydrate-containing foods like beans, grains, and vegetables.

A combination of protein with fiber-filled foods and fluid fills you up and helps you feel satisfied longer, too.

fat's story, they say. Eating a higher-fat diet may help, rather than hinder, weight loss. That's because fat differs from carbohydrate and protein in another significant way: It causes little or no rise in blood glucose levels, so it doesn't provoke insulin release into the blood after digestion. Since insulin is the designated facilitator of fat storage, low-carb proponents say a high-fat diet that's also low in carbohydrates actually prevents the body from storing glucose as fat.

keeping control

It's important to control your blood glucose concentrations. Blood glucose levels that are too low or too high make you feel tired because your cells are deprived of the energy they need to function. Chronically high glucose concentrations as seen in people with uncontrolled diabetes also damage blood vessels, particularly the very small vessels that supply the eyes and kidneys with oxygen-rich blood.

The body favors balance, and most people have a built-in mechanism that works well to keep blood glucose levels in check. It dispatches the hormone insulin from the pancreas to reduce blood glucose levels after a meal or snack containing carbohydrate or protein. Between meals, when your blood glucose levels tend to drop, the pancreas releases the hormone glucagon, which directs the liver to liberate stored glucose (glycogen). This raises your blood glucose level. Glucagon facilitates the body's production of glucose from amino acids, thereby creating an additional energy source. Insulin is also used to store any excess calories you don't burn for energy as body fat.

Low-carb diet proponents believe a diet high in carbohydrates causes weight gain and keeps you overweight because carbohydrates provoke the release of insulin into the bloodstream. Since insulin is responsible for fat storage, they say that too much insulin causes weight gain. Too much insulin coursing through your blood vessels is also unhealthy because it produces harmful changes in the vessels that supply the heart with blood, promoting heart disease.

what the research says

Low-carb eating plans produce weight loss, and that makes them popular. Despite their success, however, they are not widely accepted by the medical community. Is there a price to be paid for eating a low-carbohydrate diet? The verdict isn't in yet, but here's what we know so far.

the pros of low-carb eating

Doctors and nutritionists spent decades deriding Dr. Atkins's low-carbohydrate, high-protein, high-fat diet. Atkins, a cardiologist, maintained that his diet produced rapid weight loss and did not raise cholesterol levels, as health professionals were sure it would. Until recently, it was just the medical community's opinion against his. No independent controlled clinical trials had been done to assess the efficacy of low-carbohydrate diets at producing weight loss or to measure their effect on cholesterol levels.

That changed when the results of two controlled clinical trials were published in the *New England Journal of Medicine* in May 2003. They showed that reducing the intake of carbohydrates and increasing protein intake

could be the ticket to weight loss and weight control, at least for some people. And, much to the medical community's surprise, they also showed that low-carb diets did not cause the expected increases in blood cholesterol that can lead to heart disease. In fact, the low-carb dieters had lower levels of triglycerides (harmful blood fats that can cause a buildup of plaque in the arteries) than those who followed a low-fat diet. In addition, the low-carb dieters had higher levels of HDL (good) cholesterol than their low-fat diet counterparts.

Both of the studies compared dieters after they followed a low-carbohydrate diet with those following a more conventional low-fat, low-calorie diet. One study lasted six months, while the other lasted a year. These

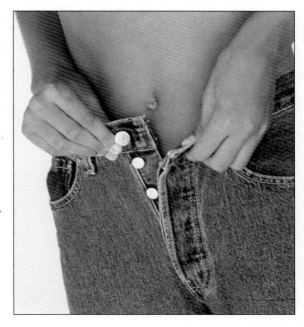

studies were some of the first to follow low-carb dieters longer than 90 days.

The six-month study followed a group of 132 severely obese men and women; half were assigned to a low-carbohydrate diet similar to the Atkins diet and half were assigned to a low-calorie, low-fat diet. Although there was a high dropout rate (about 40 percent), those who completed the study lost more weight on the low-carb diet than on the calorie- and fat-restricted diet (over six months, an average of 13 to 15 pounds compared to 4 to 7 pounds). The low-carb dieters also improved their insulin sensitivity and their triglyceride levels.

The 12-month study followed a smaller group of 63 obese men and women who were also randomly assigned to either a low-carb or a low-fat, calorie-restricted diet. The dropout rate, at 40 percent, was the same for this yearlong study. While the low-carb diet produced greater weight loss during the first six months of the study, the differences were not significant after one year. However, the low-carb diet was associated with a greater improvement in some risk factors for coronary heart disease.

Additional studies have emerged since those published in the *New England Journal of Medicine,* and they also provide some indication that low-carb dieting may be beneficial. For one year, researchers at Stanford Medical School compared the effects of four weight-loss diets with varying levels of carbohydrates among 311 overweight, premenopausal women without diabetes. In this "A to Z Weight Loss Study," participants were randomly assigned to follow the Atkins (very low carbohydrate), Zone (low carbohydrate), LEARN (Lifestyle, Exercise, Attitudes, Relationships, and Nutrition—low fat, moderate carbohydrate), or Ornish (very low fat, very high carbohydrate) diets. After one year, the women who followed the Atkins diet lost more weight and experienced more favorable changes in HDL "good" cholesterol and triglyceride concentrations compared with the other diet groups.

Another randomized trial published in 2010 involved 307 overweight adults without diabetes or cardiac risk factors and compared the effects of a low-carbohydrate diet with a low-fat diet when each was combined with a comprehensive lifestyle modification program. The low-carbohydrate group was limited to 20 grams of carbohydrates per day for the first three months with an increase of 5 grams per day each week until the desired weight was

A look at the losers

There are thousands of diets to help you lose fat. What works best? The National Weight Control Registry (NWCR) is a research project that has identified more than 5,000 people who have lost at least 30 pounds and kept the weight off for at least a year. How do they do it? About half of those followed by the NWCR lost weight on their own, while the other half used a formal weight-loss program or consulted a health professional for guidance. No matter what their method for initial weight loss, participants continue to follow a low-calorie, low-fat diet to keep the pounds off.

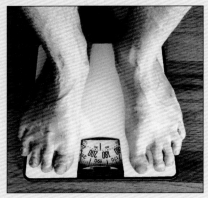

achieved. The low-fat diet allowed no more than 30 percent calories from fat and 1200 to 1800 calories per day. No differences in weight loss, body composition, or bone density were seen between the two groups during the two-year study. During the first six months, however, the low-carbohydrate diet group showed greater improvements in blood pressure and triglyceride levels. Additionally, the low-carb group had a significant increase in "good" HDL cholesterol—an approximate 23 percent increase in 2 years. This study reached two important conclusions: (1) "successful weight loss can be achieved with either a low-fat or low-carbohydrate diet when coupled with behavioral treatment," and (2) "a low-carbohydrate diet is associated with favorable changes in cardiovascular disease risk factors."

skepticism remains

Do the results of these studies mean that skeptics and critics of Atkins and other low-carb diet plans are ready to throw in the towel and join the low-carb bandwagon? Not really.

There is some evidence that a low-carb diet can preserve lean tissue while burning the fat. The idea behind any diet is loss of body fat. But restricting calories often leads to a loss of desirable lean tissue (predominantly muscle), too. Preserving lean tissue prevents a drop in metabolism (your

calorie-burning rate) because lean tissue burns more calories than fat. Curbing carbohydrate consumption may be preferable to lowering protein intake because it seems to better preserve lean tissue. Research suggests that the ratio (relationship) of carbohydrate to protein is what preserves lean tissue.

Still, health care professionals doubt the worthiness of low-carb regimens. Here's why.

overall lack of proof. Conventional wisdom says it's the total number of calories consumed that determines whether you will lose weight and that no specific distribution of carbohydrate, protein, and fat can make you lose weight faster than any other. Since carbohydrate supplies the same number of calories (four) per gram as protein and less than half the calories of a gram of fat (nine), it's counterintuitive to knock carbs as the cause for excess body fat.

Experts on the 2010 Dietary Guidelines Advisory Committee examined evidence from 36 of the most recent research articles on this topic. They concluded that diets with less than 45 percent calories from carbohydrate or more than 35 percent of calories from protein "are not more effective than other diets for weight loss or weight maintenance." They further conclude that low-carb diets "are difficult to maintain over the long term, and may be less safe."

Health professionals continue to be intrigued by newly-published studies on low-carb diets, but they want longer studies to be done. It's only after following people for many years that the true effects of eating a low-carb diet will be revealed, they say. They have lots of questions: Will the expected deleterious effects of a high-protein, high-fat diet show up later or will the decreased levels of triglycerides and increased levels of HDL (good) cholesterol found in the recently published studies continue long term? Will following a high-protein diet for years eventually damage the kidneys, promote the formation of kidney stones, and lead to gout, as some evidence indicates? Will a low-carb diet cause osteoporosis? And what about the brain, which relies on glucose to work efficiently? Will there be harm to brain function over the long haul? The medical community is waiting for the answers to these questions before it gives its verdict on low-carb dieting.

safety concerns. Any diet can be dangerous when it severely restricts calorie and nutrient intake, intentionally or not. Nausea, dizziness, constipation, fatigue, dehydration, bad breath, and appetite loss are among the

reported effects of very-low carbohydrate diets. Even the less extreme low-carb plans may be unsafe because they restrict certain foods that help fight disease. For example, going without the recommended three servings of low-fat dairy foods for months or years means losing out on bone-building calcium and vitamin D. Consuming fewer than the five to nine suggested servings of fruits and vegetables (combined) leads to reduced intakes of beneficial antioxidant vitamins and phytonutrients, compounds found only in plant foods and considered valuable weapons in the battle against heart disease and cancer. And foregoing whole grains may increase your chances of developing diabetes and heart disease.

stick-to-it-ability. Both of the studies published in the *New England Journal of Medicine* had a high dropout rate—about 40 percent. These studies were only 6 or 12 months long, which doesn't bode well for the ability of dieters to stick with a low-carb regimen for the long term. The challenge of any diet is not just to help people lose weight but to make the lifelong changes in eating that will keep the weight off for good. Longer studies are needed to determine whether a low-carb diet can be a satisfactory way of life, one that leads to permanent weight loss.

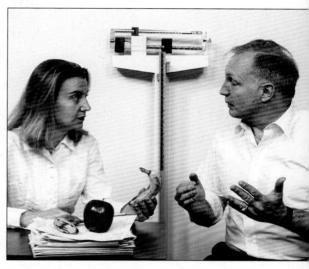

looking to the future

Low-carb diets, once the stepchild of the diet and health community, are finally getting the attention and scrutiny they deserve. That's great, since dieters have been experimenting with low-carb eating for several decades. But we still need the results of carefully constructed, long-running studies to make a final determination on the effectiveness of low-carb dieting and its impact on health. In the meantime, it's unlikely that low-carb diets are harmful for most healthy people for a short period of time. But if you do go low carb, make sure you check with a health professional who will monitor your blood cholesterol levels and your bone mass and will check to make sure you are not developing kidney stones. Depending on the severity of your low-carb regimen, your health provider should also give you guidance about vitamin, mineral, and fiber supplementation.

are low-carb diets for everyone?

Everyone can cut refined carbs

Even if you have a health condition that makes a strict low-carb diet unwise, much of the advice in this book is still valuable. Everyone can benefit from cutting back on "empty" carbs—the ones that come in foods such as cookies, white bread, bagels, and donuts—and empty calories. You'll need to check with your doctor first, but chances are you'll get the green light to trim refined carbs and add whole grains, fruits, and vegetables to your diet.

It's unlikely that any single type of diet is ideal for everyone. But low-carb diets can be particularly risky for certain groups of people. Here's how to decide whether you are in a high-risk group.

Low-carb diets are, by definition, high in protein, high in fat, or both. The protein content of the eating plan proposed by Dr. Atkins, as well as those in the *Protein Power LifePlan, the New Sugar Busters!,* and *the Zone* diets, is almost twice the Recommended Dietary Allowance of 50 grams for adult women and 63 grams for adult men. Why is that problematic? Some health conditions make it more difficult to process the additional protein consumed in a low-carb diet, and others require a higher volume of carbohydrates to maintain good health.

processing protein

Eating extra protein places a burden on the liver and kidneys. Your body doesn't store protein directly, so these organs work harder to process it. The liver and kidneys are responsible for ridding the body of uric acid and ammonia, the substances that are left after the body digests protein. If you have a health condition that compromises the kidneys or liver, then you should not try a low-carb, high-protein diet. Since the liver and kidneys also process medications, be sure to check with your physician before starting a high-protein diet if you take any medication regularly. The additional protein could jeopardize your liver and kidney function.

diabetes and high blood pressure. People with diabetes and high blood pressure are at greater risk for kidney disease and are especially vulnerable to the detrimental effects of consuming large amounts of protein. And those with high blood pressure may also be compromised by the diuretic effects of ketosis.

gout. If you're prone to gout, bypass protein-packed diets. Uric acid—a product of protein breakdown—can cause or aggravate gout, an arthritis-type condition characterized by painful uric acid deposits in the joints.

osteoporosis. Excess protein may also be harmful to bones, increasing your risk for osteoporosis, a bone disease that mostly strikes women after menopause but has its beginnings much earlier in life. In response to the acid environment produced by excessive protein intake, your kidneys direct bones to release calcium to buffer the acid. This can leach calcium from the bones if you don't eat a calcium and potassium-rich diet or take a supplement of these nutrients. Eating plenty of potassium-packed fruits and vegetables can counteract calcium loss because potassium also buffers acid. Getting at least 1,000 milligrams of calcium daily will help offset the calcium-wasting effects of protein, too. However, some low-carb diets tend to fall short in potassium and calcium because they restrict carbohydrate foods that are rich in these nutrients. The Paleo diet, for instance, prohibits all dairy products. Other diet plans forbid or drastically restrict dairy products during certain phases, which can stretch into long periods of time and that you would return to intermittently.

pregnancy and childhood. Pregnant and lactating women and growing children should also steer clear of low-carb diets because they limit foods that foster a child's growth and development and may not satisfy energy and nutrient needs. In addition, too much protein in the diet puts unnecessary strain on a child's developing kidneys.

heart disease and cancer. Some low-carb diets don't restrict protein, fat, or calories. So while you're whittling your waistline, you could be clogging your arteries and increasing your cancer risk. This is especially true if you favor foods higher in total and saturated fat, such as meat, cheese, and cream, over lower-fat, high-protein choices including poultry, seafood, and low-fat yogurt. Unrestricted consumption of animal foods that are rich in total fat, saturated fat, and cholesterol, including meat and cheese, raises low-density lipoprotein (LDL, bad cholesterol), an effect compounded by the relative absence of high-carbohydrate, high-fiber plant foods such as whole grains, fruits, and vegetables, which help keep blood lipids in check. Diets high in red meat and low in fiber may increase cancer risk. And low-carb diets miss many fruits, vegetables, and whole grains that provide cancer-fighting phytochemicals.

Turn down the heat

Low-carb diets pack a lot of protein-rich animal foods, which can increase your risk for cancer, depending on how you cook them. According to the National Cancer Institute, cooking beef, pork, poultry, and fish at high temperatures creates chemicals called heterocyclic amines (HCA) that may increase cancer risk. Frying, broiling, and grilling produce the largest amounts of HCAs. Baking, steaming, and roasting produce the least. Meats that are partially cooked in a microwave oven before cooking by other methods also have lower levels of HCAs.

the carbohydrate addict's diet

About the authors

Richard F. Heller, M.S, Ph.D. is Professor Emeritus at City University in New York (CUNY). His wife and professional partner, Rachael F. Heller, M.A, M.Ph., Ph.D., is a retired assistant professor in the Department of Biomedical Sciences at CUNY. Both were overweight as children and young adults and developed the Carbohydrate Addicts Diet after failing countless times at weight loss through "conventional" means. They reportedly lost a combined 200 pounds with this plan and have stayed within their respective normal weights for the past two decades. Their most recent book, *The 7-Day Low-Carb Rescue and Recovery Plan*, was published in 2004.

the basic idea

Most people who are overweight suffer from an addiction to carbohydrates, according to the Hellers. They say carbohydrate addiction is a genetically determined disorder caused by an imbalance in body chemistry. Being overweight, then, is no more the carbohydrate addict's fault than is an illness such as epilepsy, and it's not something that can be solved by willpower. It can only be handled by regulating and restricting the intake of carbohydrates.

Those who have this disorder, say the Hellers, overproduce insulin in response to eating carbohydrates. Here's what happens: When you consume carbohydrates, your body releases far more insulin than it needs to move glucose (blood sugar) into your cells for energy. When too much insulin is in the blood, your brain fails to get the message that you are no longer hungry. You don't feel satisfied and most likely will want to eat again soon. Carbohydrate addicts may recognize that their compulsion to eat again right after they finish a meal or snack is illogical, but they can't resist the drive. Carbohydrate addicts never truly feel satisfied, so they repeatedly overeat and find it impossible to lose weight, according to the Hellers.

The Hellers believe that conventional low-fat, high-carb diet plans don't work for carbohydrate addicts because these diets encourage eating carbohydrate several times a day. Even small amounts of carbohydrate can send a carbohydrate addict into the downward spiral of overeating and weight gain, say these authors.

how the plan works

The Carbohydrate Addict's Diet does not require calorie counting, and you don't need to keep track of grams of carbohydrate, fat, or protein. There are a few rules that dieters must adhere to, however. Carbohydrate consumption is restricted to a single "reward" meal each day. That meal must include equal portions of nonstarchy carbohydrates such as salad greens, protein, and starchy carbohydrates such as bread and pasta——all of which must be consumed within one hour. You can have as many servings as you want during that one hour, but you must maintain the same proportions. Your other two meals must be free of starchy carbohydrates: They can include only protein and nonstarchy vegetables.

During the Entry Plan, which lasts for two weeks and is designed for weight loss, you're allowed two low-carbohydrate meals and one Reward Meal a day. After the two-week period, you can choose from four different plans (A, B, C, or D), depending on your weight-loss goal. Each plan is based on the Entry Plan and includes one Reward Meal. In fact, the Entry Plan and Plan B are identical. Plan A is the same as the Entry Plan plus a low-carb snack. Plan C adds a salad to the reward meal, and Plan D encourages you to skip one low-carb meal a day and add a salad at your Reward Meal.

The Reward Meal may come as a surprise to professed carbohydrate

addicts because it may include any food you want in any amount, including alcohol and dessert, as long as it is balanced proportionally to the other foods you eat at that meal. But the Hellers say that restricting the meal to 60 minutes limits insulin release into the bloodstream, no matter what you're eating. While they do encourage a wide variety of healthy foods for your Reward Meal, the Hellers believe there is no reason to forego favorite foods. It's up to you whether your Reward Meal is for breakfast, lunch, or dinner.

unique features
The premise behind The Carbohydrate Addict's Diet is that carbohydrates are addictive substances that encourage dependence and produce a habitual or excessive need to eat them. The Hellers give a detailed portrait of the characteristics of carbohydrate addicts and offer a test for you to take to find out whether you suffer from carbohydrate addiction. You're allowed just one meal rich in carbohydrates each day.

Carbohydrate, protein, and fat allowances

- There are no set guidelines for the amount of carbohydrate, protein, or fat in your diet. But high-carbohydrate foods must be confined to a single meal that lasts no more than 60 minutes.

Meal plan/ recipes

- Twelve days of low-carbohydrate menus are included, as is a chapter of low-carb recipes.

the new atkins for a new you

About the authors

Dr. Stephen D. Phinney, Dr. Jeff S. Volek, and Dr. Eric Westman collaborated to write this newest update to the low-carb diet first espoused almost 40 years ago by the late Robert Atkins, M.D. Dr. Phinney received his medical degree from Stanford University and has a Ph.D. in nutritional biochemistry from MIT. He chairs the Atkins Science Advisory Board. Dr. Jeff Volek is an associate professor and researcher in the Department of Kinesiology at the University of Connecticut. Dr. Westman is an associate professor of medicine at Duke University Health System.

the basic idea

People are overweight because they are fighting a "metabolic bully" caused by consuming too many carbohydrates, according to these Atkins promoters. Years of eating too many carbs, they say, can make your body's insulin—the hormone that moderates your glucose level—less effective (see box on page 11 for an explanation of insulin resistance). To deal with rising blood sugars, your pancreas overproduces insulin after a high-carb meal or snack. Excessive insulin promotes fat storage and prevents your body from burning off fat, dooming you to be heavy. But you can stimulate your body to burn more fat, say these authors, by eating a very low carbohydrate diet.

The Atkins plan claims to turn your body into "a fat-burning machine" through a diet composed primarily of protein, fat, and fiber. Its core premise is to limit sugars and other refined carbohydrates so that your body produces less insulin and begins to burn fat rather than carbohydrate as its primary energy source.

For Atkins, lipolysis—or fat breakdown—is the goal. When there isn't enough glucose to burn for energy, the liver turns to protein and fat. It converts fat to acid-type substances called ketones to provide fuel for the body. An accumulation of ketones in the blood or urine is called ketosis or ketonuria—an abnormal metabolic condition caused by consuming an inadequate supply of carbohydrates to meet your energy needs. Stimulating lipolysis on a very low-carbohydrate diet suppresses your appetite and breaks the cycle of excess insulin in the bloodstream that promotes fat storage, according to Atkins diet proponents. They dismiss the dangers of ketosis in healthy people, saying the risks are overrated by the medical profession. To make sure you're burning fat, Atkins recommends urine testing for what he calls "nutritional ketosis," which most health professionals would call "starvation ketosis."

the plan

The Atkins Nutritional Approach requires no calorie counting but recommends being "sensible, not obsessive" about portions. The theory is that as long as you choose from the acceptable foods, steering clear of most carbohydrates, you will lose weight.

The plan consists of four phases:

Phase 1 (Induction) lasts for two weeks or more, until you are burning primarily fat for energy. You're limited to no more than 20 grams of Net Carbs (total carbs minus fiber) a day. For example, a salad of 1 cup Romaine lettuce, 1 cup broccoli, 1 whole avocado, and 1 tomato contains approximately 13 grams of Net Carbs, according to Atkins' list of acceptable foods.

Phase 2 (Ongoing Weight Loss, or OWL) lasts from two weeks to two months or until you are within 10 pounds of your goal weight. During this phase, you increase your daily Net Carb intake to 25 grams and can add 5 grams of Net Carbs to your daily intake each week as long as you continue to lose weight. Weight loss during OWL is more gradual, but if your weight loss plateaus, you decrease your carbohydrate intake. OWL's goal is to find the number of Net Carbs you can eat each day and still continue to lose weight.

Phase 3 (Pre-maintenance) may last for a few weeks to several months. During this phase, you slowly lose your last 10 pounds. You add 10 grams of Net Carbs to your daily intake each week or every other week until your weight loss is as little as ½ pound per week. When you reach your goal weight, you are directed to find your Atkins Carbohydrate Equilibrium (ACE), which is the number of Net Carbs you can eat daily without gaining or losing weight.

Phase 4 is Lifetime Maintenance. You stick with your ACE number and stay within five pounds of your new weight.

unique features

The Atkins Nutritional Approach is very low in carbohydrate (estimated range: 20 to 90 grams, or as low at 5 percent of your daily calorie needs), perhaps the lowest of any low-carb eating regimen. (The 2010 Dietary Guidelines for Americans recommends getting 45 to 65 percent of daily calories from carbohydrate, which amounts to 225 to 325 grams of carbohydrate per day.) After initially cutting carbohydrate intake to 20 grams a day, you gradually increase carbohydrate intake until you reach your weight-loss goal and learn the amount of carbohydrate you can eat every day without gaining weight. Ketosis is encouraged and seen as a sign of fat-burning success.

This newest Atkins diet has been modified from the original Atkins plan to reflect emerging nutritional science, particularly the need to eat a sufficient amount of fruits and vegetables, and to reduce the symptoms of "the Atkins flu" (headaches, dizziness, weakness and fatigue), as well as leg cramps and constipation that often accompany the conversion to a low-carb diet.

Exercise is an integral part of the Atkins program. Nutritional supplements, including a daily multivitamin and omega 3s, are recommended.

Carbohydrate, protein, and fat allowances

- Carbohydrate: 20 grams "Net Carbs" a day in the Induction phase, gradually increasing until you reach your Atkins Carbohydrate Equilibrium (ACE) to maintain weight loss.
- Protein: No set protein allowances. Recommended 4–8 ounces protein foods at each meal; cheese is limited to 3 to 4 ounces daily because of its carb content (about 1 gram per ounce.)
- Fat: No set fat allowances.

Meal plan/recipes

- Includes several dozen recipes and meal plans for each phase of the diet, including vegetarian options.

the new sugar busters!
cut sugar to trim fat

About the authors

Morrison C. Bethea, M.D., is a thoracic, cardiac, and vascular surgeon in New Orleans and is a diplomat of the American Board of Thoracic Surgery. Sam S. Andrews, M.D., is an endocrinologist who specializes in obesity treatment and currently practices medicine with the Audubon Internal Medicine Group in New Orleans, LA. He is a former associate professor of medicine at the Louisiana State University Medical School in New Orleans. Luis A. Balart, M.D., is the chief of gastroenterology and hepatology at Tulane University School of Medicine. H. Leighton Steward is an Emeritus Trustee of Tulane University and has been CEO of a Fortune 500 energy company.

the basic idea

Sugar is not inherently "toxic", say these authors, but consuming refined sugar, such as sucrose (table sugar), corn syrup, molasses, and honey, is certainly toxic to many people, especially those with diabetes. And sugar makes many people obese, especially refined sugars that cause a significant spike in insulin levels. There is nothing good about high levels of insulin in the body, according to the authors. Insulin causes the body to store excess sugar as fat and prevents the body from burning stored fat. It also stimulates the liver to make more cholesterol.

In this updated version of the original Sugar Busters!, the authors recommend that you eat the way your ancestors ate (until very recently): Your diet should exclude all refined sugar and include only whole-grain and unrefined foods. You must virtually eliminate from your diet white potatoes, white rice, refined bread, corn products, beets, and all refined sugars such as sucrose (table sugar), corn syrup, molasses, and honey. Sugared soft drinks and beer are also banned.

The authors do not call the Sugar Busters! plan a low-carbohydrate diet. They consider it simply a "correct carbohydrate lifestyle"—one that is made of foods that are low in sugar, low on the glycemic index, and high in fiber. They say that medical studies are proving that this type of diet is good for weight control and the control of many maladies of our modern society.

the plan

Sugar Busters! does not put you through a crash or "deprivation" phase like many other diets do. Instead, the authors tell you to "start out like you can hold out"—with an eating pattern that you can maintain for the rest of your life. To guide you, Sugar Busters! lays down the rules: Eliminate all refined sugars and starches; eat lean meats, poultry, and seafood; limit foods rich in saturated and trans fat; and eat only dairy products that have no added sugar. Eat either three full meals plus appropriate snacks (such as whole

fruit or nuts) or six small meals a day—and don't eat after 8:00 P.M. There are two simple rules about portion size: Don't overfill your plate, and don't go back for seconds. They advise you to drink between six and eight glasses of water every day. Alcohol is limited to moderate levels; the best choice, they say, is red wine because of its cardiovascular benefits. Beer is forbidden.

Sugar Busters! claims to be nutritionally adequate because it allows a healthy mix of foods from all food groups; that's why it does not recommend supplements like many other diet plans do. Moderate regular exercise is also recommended.

unique features

Sugar Busters! details in easily understood terms how digestion and metabolism work, and it helps dieters relate these processes to the issues of insulin levels and health.

The diet's major goal is disease prevention, but it also stresses weight control and weight loss if you are overweight. The book contains chapters on women and weight loss; preventing childhood obesity; and how the Sugar Busters! diet helps head off and manage diabetes and heart disease.

The plan recommends eating fruit by itself and has some food-combining rules. It also recommends limiting fluids at meals and snacks to promote proper chewing and to prevent the dilution of digestive enzymes.

Carbohydrate, protein, and fat allowances

- Carbohydrate: No set allowances, but averages at least 40 percent of calories.
- Protein: No set allowances, but averages 30 percent of calories.
- Fat: No set fat allowances, but averages 30 percent of calories.

Meal plan/recipes

- No meal plans. Includes dozens of recipes.

the paleo diet
lose weight and get healthy by eating the foods
you were designed to eat

the basic idea

The Paleo (Old Stone Age) Diet is not just another low-carbohydrate diet, according to Loren Cordain; it is the diet that human beings are genetically adapted to eat. He believes that our current "healthy" diet wreaks havoc with our Paleolithic constitution, and so the way to lose weight and regain our well-being is to eat the way our hunter-gatherer ancestors ate 333 generations ago.

Cordain's diet plan is composed of approximately half animal and half plant foods. Compared with conventional diets, it provides a greater percentage of protein (up to 34 percent of calories) and fat (as high as 44 percent of daily calories) and a lower percentage of carbohydrate (22 to 40 percent of calories) than conventional diets.

Cordain advocates eating the way ancient humans ate: Their diet consisted of lean meats (including wild game), fish, seafood, and as much fruit and nonstarchy vegetables as they wanted. Although he believes this diet is not fanatically strict, it prohibits cereals, legumes, and dairy foods. According to Cordain, archeological records show that when ancient humans sowed seeds, they harvested health problems, including a short stature. As a result, he believes that grains are inferior foods that are not good for you. Cordain quotes studies showing that some B vitamins (such as biotin) are poorly absorbed from grains and that excessive consumption of wheat and corn contribute to B-vitamin deficiency diseases such as pellagra and beriberi. Lean meats, he points out, are excellent sources of these vitamins.

Legumes, he says, contain "antinutrients" that prevent the body from absorbing the proper nutrients and disrupt the acid balance in the kidneys.

Ancient people did not drink milk and yet they got enough calcium from fruits and vegetables to build strong bones. We should do that, too, says Cordain.

The Paleo Diet also restricts processed and other high-sodium foods since these were not part of the prehistoric human menu either.

Cordain advocates physical activity for weight loss and health and includes a chapter on "Paleo exercise" that

About the author

Loren Cordain, Ph.D., is a professor in the Health and Exercise Science Department at Colorado State University. He is acknowledged as a leading expert on the Paleolithic (a time period approximately 2.5 million years ago) diet and has written several articles in scientific journals on this topic.

follows the example of natural hunter-gatherer activities.

how the plan works

You cannot overeat on this diet, Cordain says, so calories are not restricted. The diet is high in protein, fruits, and vegetables, with moderate amounts of fat, especially healthful omega-3 and monounsaturated fats. Weight loss occurs because protein has a higher "thermic effect" (it revs up metabolism when you eat) than fat or carbohydrate. High-protein diets also help control your appetite, says Cordain.

There are three different levels of adherence, depending on how strict you want to be and how quickly you want to lose weight. Entry Level 1: For two to four weeks, you follow an 85/15 rule. For 85 percent of your meals, you stick to the Paleo diet; 15 percent of your meals (approximately 3 meals a week) are "open" (you can cheat a bit).

Maintenance Level 2 allows only a 90/10 split. Two meals a week are open (you can eat whatever you like) and the rest are strictly comprised of Paleo foods. Maximal Weight Loss is achieved at Level 3, says the author. This is the most restrictive level, in which you follow the Paleo plan 95 percent of the time and are allowed just 1 open meal per week.

Cordain includes diet analyses showing that the Paleo Diet can pro-vide 100 percent of your daily nutrient requirements. A Stone Age diet, he contends, is rich in vitamins, minerals, and phytochemicals (plant-based substances) that contribute to good health.

unique features

The book, *The Paleo Diet,* reads much like an anthropology lesson, and the author provides extensive information about the lifestyle of ancient humans and the evolution of food production. He includes a long list of supporting references—including articles he has published on this subject in various nutrition journals. A companion book, *The Paleo Diet Cookbook,* published in 2011, helps dieters learn to cook the Paleo way.

Carbohydrate, protein, and fat allowances

- There are no set carbohydrate, protein, or fat allowances, but the emphasis is on lean meats and healthy fats.

Meal plan/ recipes

- Includes sample meal plans for all three levels of the diet plus an entire chapter of recipes.

the protein power lifeplan

the basic idea

The goal of the Protein Power LifePlan is to reintroduce you to your hunting past and make a strong case for eating meat. It's not impossible to stick to the Eadeses' plan if you're a vegetarian; it just takes more effort.

Though health experts disagree with their premise, the Eadeses believe our modern lifestyle has deviated from our ancestral one to the point where we are squandering our health. Our diet has changed radically, but our physiology has evolved imperceptibly, they say. We are nothing more than cavemen in designer suits with cell phones.

The shift away from meat to a grain-based diet has been our undoing, say the Eadeses. Fossil records show that human health, height, and longevity declined after the development of agriculture.

Why are grains so troubling? Their carbohydrate content, of course. The Eadeses argue that about 75 percent of adults overproduce insulin in response to carbohydrate consumption. A diet rich in sugar and starches (the typical American eating pattern) causes insulin overload in the bloodstream. This is the primary reason for the "diseases of civilization": heart disease, diabetes, high blood pressure, and elevated cholesterol and triglycerides in the blood, along with an array of other harmful conditions.

A high-carbohydrate, low-fat diet is not the panacea that health professionals had hoped for, the authors say. Low-fat eating has not diminished the cluster of disorders caused by excess insulin. Eating more fat may be part of the answer, but the Eadeses caution that all fat is not created equal. We may have evolved on a fat-packed diet, but our ancestors ate healthier fats, including the omega-3 kind found in seafood and in the fat of game animals. In addition, modern man consumes harmful trans fat, the type found in processed foods.

Reducing carbohydrate may be the primary route to better health, but the authors take a more holistic approach. They concede that decreased caloric intake also works to reduce insulin levels in the blood but note that it's not nearly as effective as curbing carbohydrate consumption. They prescribe exercise, arguing that our ancient ancestors were lean, fit, and strong-boned. Stone Age exercise consisted of bursts of high-intensity activities that

About the authors

Michael R. Eades, M.D., and Mary Dan Eades, M.D., the husband-and-wife team that wrote *Protein Power,* used to be in private practice, specializing in bariatric medicine. They currently write, lecture, and pursue research in metabolic and nutritional medicine. They are the authors of 14 books, including *The 30-Day Low-Carb Diet Solution* and *The 6-Week Cure for the Middle-Aged Middle.*

used the large muscle groups, followed by long sedentary periods. To that end, the Eadeses have designed a caveman-like activity regimen that includes stretching, sprinting, leaping, and jumping.

Nutrient supplements and prescription medication, as needed, are also part of their multifaceted program.

how the plan works

You begin by determining your protein and carbohydrate requirements. Detailed charts, based on height and weight, are provided to help you. The Eadeses recommend that everyone start at the Intervention level for carbohydrate, which allows less than 40 grams of Effective Carbohydrate Content (ECC)—the total carbohydrate content of a food minus the fiber content—per day. Fiber is subtracted from the total carb content because fiber is not digested nor converted to glucose. The authors provide a chart of the ECC for common foods and teach you how to evaluate the ECC of packaged foods. The Intervention level lasts from a few weeks to several months, depending on your health and weight. Next is the Transition level for carbohydrate intake for one to two months, then to the Maintenance level forever. Each successive level allows more carbohydrate.

Once you know your protein and carbohydrate requirements, you may choose a nutritional plan based on three levels of restriction:

Hedonist: The least restrictive regimen that allows limited quantities of added sugars.

Dilettante: Avoids processed meats, most grains, and sweeteners and encourages organic dairy products.

Purist: Closest to a truly Paleolithic diet, this level prohibits all grains, dairy products, processed foods, sugars (except honey, which was available to prehistoric man), artificial sweeteners, coffee, tea, and other caffeine sources, and all alcohol. Only organic fruits and vegetables and natural (antibiotic-, hormone-, and pesticide-free) meat, poultry, and game are allowed.

At every stage of the eating plan, you are encouraged to drink 64 ounces of filtered water daily.

unique features

The Eadeses use a sophisticated and sometimes complicated approach to low-carb eating. The eating plan can be difficult to figure out on your own. The authors provide in-depth explanations for their theories, using complex biochemical, physiological, and anthropological information. Each chapter provides a Bottom Line summary at the end that highlights the main points. The plan promotes supplemental magnesium, chromium picolinate, alpha lipoic acid, and coenzyme Q10 to improve insulin receptor function.

Carbohydrate, protein, and fat allowances

- Carbohydrate: Intake is based on your current state of health, level of physical activity, and whether you need to lose weight. Everyone should start with the Intervention level of carbohydrate restriction, a maximum of 40 grams per day.

- Protein: Minimum requirements per meal vary with weight and height.

- Fat: Varies based on weight loss or maintenance goals. The authors recommend cutting back on fatty foods if you're not losing weight or if you start gaining. The plan encourages unsaturated fats and discourages most vegetable cooking oils and trans fat.

Meal plan/ recipes

- Provides meal plans that account for your chosen carbohydrate intake and commitment level.

the schwarzbein principle II
the transition

About the author

Dr. Diana Schwarz-bein is an endocrinologist and the founder of The Endocrinology Institute of Santa Barbara, where she specializes in metabolic healing, diabetes, osteoporosis, menopause, and thyroid disorders. Through her work with people with type 2 diabetes, Schwarzbein became frustrated when she found that the high-carbohydrate, low-fat diets routinely prescribed to manage diabetes made the condition worse.

the basic idea

Dr. Diana Schwarzbein's defining principle is that your diet and lifestyle habits determine your "metabolic age" and predict your overall health. To achieve your ideal body composition, you will need to go through what she calls "the transition" in order to restore your metabolism and rebalance your hormones. This is done in four stages, and the goal is to become "insulin sensitive"—when all the functions of insulin are working correctly. Insulin resistance (IR), she explains, occurs when cells resist insulin's command to allow glucose to enter. When cells fail to respond to insulin, the pancreas pumps out more of this hormone until the level of insulin in the blood can finally overwhelm the cells' resistance. IR means that you have higher insulin levels in the bloodstream, which Schwarzbein says are initially protective but later lead to diseases of aging such as high cholesterol, high blood pressure, and type 2 diabetes. When you balance your hormones (namely, insulin) you will heal your metabolism and lose weight, Schwarzbein says.

She contends that sugars are more damaging to your body than fats or insulin, since they promote high insulin levels. She therefore advocates a nutritionally healthy diet based on the "Schwarzbein Square," which includes Healthy Proteins, Nonstarchy vegetables, Healthy Fats, and "Real" Carbohydrates (organic foods that can be grown, picked, or harvested). Additional components of her plan are stress management (which includes getting enough sleep); avoidance of caffeine, alcohol, and other "toxic chemicals;" cross-training exercises; and hormone replacement therapy if needed. Schwarzbein believes your body will begin to burn fat after your hormones are normalized. "You need to be healthy to lose weight, not lose weight to be healthy," she explains. Schwarzbein warns readers that "there are no short cuts" to healing a badly damaged metabolism.

the plan

The ultimate goal of Schwarzbein's plan is to normalize how insulin functions in the body. There are no calorie limits, although Schwarzbein recommends avoiding certain foods, such as milk because it contains "hidden sugar" in the form of lactose. If you are insulin sensitive (i.e. your hormones are normalized), you can drink milk in moderation (1 to 2 cups a day). Protein should be the main nutrient at each meal, and "man-made" or refined grain products like pasta, white rice, flour tortillas, and desserts are off-limits.

The first stage of the Schwarzbein Principle II Program (SPII) helps you pinpoint your metabolic type so you can begin to become insulin sensitive and develop healthy adrenal glands. Stage 2 is the healing phase, in which the body repairs itself after years of damage from poor nutrition and lifestyle habits. Your meal plan is based on your metabolic type and includes anywhere from 15 to 45 grams of carbohydrates per meal. You enter Stage 3—the fat-burning phase—after your hormones are normalized and your metabolism is healed. You reach Stage 4—the healed stage—when your hormones are balanced and you have achieved your "ideal body composition."

unique features

This diet focuses on correcting metabolic disturbances to reduce body fat and avoid premature aging and the diseases associated with it, including heart disease and cancer. A healthy lifestyle is emphasized along with a low-carb diet. Schwarzbein encourages consumption of healthy fats—those that do not have any "damaged fat," such as trans fat. Monounsaturated or polyunsaturated fats are better than saturated fat as long as they contain no trans fat, says Schwarzbein. She warns dieters to avoid foods that contain damaged fats, chemicals, or sugar, such as bottled salad dressings or processed meats.

Carbohydrate, protein, and fat allowances

- Carbohydrate: Intake is matched to your metabolism type; between 15 to 45 grams per meal.
- Protein: 1.0 to 1.2 grams per kg actual weight
- Fat: No limit on fat consumption, but avoid unhealthy "damaged" fats, i.e. trans fats

Meal plans/ recipes

- Provides sample meal plans for 15, 30, and 45 grams of carbohydrate per meal, as well as recipes.

the south beach diet supercharged

About the author

Arthur Agatston, M.D., is a preventive cardiologist and associate professor of medicine at the University of Miami Miller School of Medicine. He helped pioneer a method for scoring coronary calcium, a method currently used to predict heart disease. Agatston has published more than 100 scientific articles and has served on the board of the American Dietetic Association Foundation. In 1995, he developed the South Beach diet to help his patients with heart disease and diabetes lose weight and improve their blood cholesterol and glucose levels.

the basic idea

In this updated version of the original South Beach diet book, the basic principles remain unchanged, although Dr. Arthur Agatston puts more emphasis on exercise and introduces what he calls a unique metabolism-revving program based on the science of interval training and core functional fitness. Carbohydrates, particularly the highly processed kind, are responsible for most of our excess girth, Agatston says, and the type of carbohydrate you eat matters because carbs influence food cravings that make you gain weight. Carbohydrates also affect insulin levels in the bloodstream. When the bloodstream receives an infusion of glucose after eating foods that cause rapid spikes in blood glucose, including white bread, potatoes, and cookies, the pancreas responds by releasing a great deal of insulin. But when you eat carbohydrates that are metabolized more slowly, such as high-fiber vegetables and unprocessed whole grains, insulin release is gradual. As a result, he says, food cravings and blood concentrations of glucose and insulin are better controlled, making it easier to lose weight and keep it off.

With the South Beach Diet, it's possible to correct the way you respond to the foods that caused you to pack on the pounds in the first place (i.e. "bad" carbohydrates). Not only will you lose weight, but Agatston claims you will alter your body chemistry to decrease the risk of diabetes, heart disease, and polycystic ovary syndrome, a condition that affects fertility.

Agatston maintains this is not a high-protein, low-carbohydrate diet; nor is it a low-fat diet. He calls it a nutritionally sound diet that consists of a wide variety of wholesome foods. Nevertheless, the first two weeks of the South Beach diet eliminate most sources of carbohydrate.

Agatston also emphasizes eating healthy fats by encouraging a diet with lots of seafood, olive oil, nuts, and avocados. He says the problem with some low-carbohydrate diets is that they are packed with saturated fat that harms your arteries and causes them to narrow, which blocks blood flow to major organs. High-fat meals can also trigger a heart attack in some people, Agatston asserts.

the plan

Agatston says the South Beach Supercharged diet is "a diet you can live with." In this new edition, he places more emphasis on recognizing good and bad carbohydrates rather than their glycemic index (GI) rating. You are not required to count calories, and there are no limits on allowed foods. The plan has three phases.

Phase One: For the first two weeks, you eat healthy lean protein, vegetables, salads, beans, legumes, nuts, eggs, and low-fat dairy foods to jumpstart weight loss and minimize food cravings. Good fats such as extra virgin olive oil and canola oils are also allowed. No bread, rice, potatoes, pasta, fruit, juice, or refined sugars are allowed in this phase.

Phase Two: You can begin here if you have less than 10 pounds to lose, says Agatston. During this phase, you can begin to reintroduce foods that were "off limits" in Phase 1. But make sure they are "good" carbohydrates such as whole fruit, whole-grain breads and pasta, and some starchy vegetables such as sweet potatoes. Red or white wine is also allowed occasionally during this phase. Your goal during this second phase is to eat more good carbohydrate—those that are nutrient-rich and high in fiber—while continuing to shed pounds until you hit your weight target. You shouldn't go overboard on good carbohydrate foods

either, says Agatston, because large portions will produce higher-than-desired blood glucose levels.

Phase Three begins when you reach your healthy weight. No food in this phase is completely off-limits, says Agatston, as long as you understand how to make good food choices. A brief chapter in the book explains how to enjoy the South Beach Diet for life after reaching your weight goal.

unique features

While the glycemic index was the cornerstone of the original South Beach diet plan, Agatston's recommendations in this book hinge on "good" carbohydrates—those that are rich in nutrients and fiber. The ultimate goal is to arrive at a carbohydrate intake that allows you to maintain your weight for a lifetime.

A good portion of this edition features a "Supercharged Fitness Program" consisting of interval walking and total body workout exercises, which you do on alternate days. The book includes weekly exercise plans for all three phases of the diet.

Carbohydrate, protein, and fat allowances

- There are no set carbohydrate, protein, or fat allowances.

Meal plan/ recipes

- Includes two weeks of sample recipes and menu plans for Phases 1 and 2 of the diet. Lists of foods to enjoy and those to avoid or eat rarely are also included.

suzanne somers' sexy forever
how to fight fat after forty

the basic idea

In her latest weight-loss book, Suzanne Somers offers a lifelong program for health and fitness, targeting people over 40. The key to losing weight after the age of 40, she says, is to understand the ubiquity of toxins—such as white flour and sugar—in our food and environment. These toxins slow your metabolism and cause you to get fat, she claims. Somers blames a variety of health problems, from asthma and fatigue to serious digestive problems, on the toxic environment in which we live.

She also blames weight gain on imbalances of hormones such as insulin.

You can balance your hormones and speed weight loss by cleaning out the chemicals and toxins in your body, Somers says. Her plan begins with a "Detox Phase" to get rid of these unhealthy substances. It then moves into a weight-loss phase. After you reach your goal weight and elminate toxins from your cells, you enter the maintenance phase.

Basic to Somer's plan is the elimination of foods that raise insulin levels such as sugar, refined starches, starchy vegetables, and alcohol, as well as bad fats such as trans fats. Vegetable oils made from corn, cottonseed, peanut, safflower, and sunflower are also eliminated. The best oils, she says, are olive, flaxseed, fish, and perilla (an herb from the mint family).

Her plan also calls for eating only clean organic food that is free of chemicals, toxins, fillers, and preservatives.

Somers continues to recommend eating certain foods with others: proteins with healthy fat and low-starch vegetables, for example. Fruit should be eaten on an empty stomach to maximize digestion and nutrient absorption. And if you switch from a carbohydrate meal to one that contains protein and healthy fats, you should wait 2 hours between any meal or snack.

Her plan calls for 3 meals a day, including only approved nutrient-rich carbohydrate foods in specific portions at certain meals. Lists of approved foods are provided in her book.

how the plan works

Somers recommends a diet of foods that are low on the glycemic index (GI) because they will release stored energy from your fat cells. And she suggests that you eat 9 grams of protein for every 20 pounds of body weight, which is similar to the average amount of protein recommended for nondieters. However, she also suggests that you eat 6 to 8 ounces of protein at every meal, which is twice the amount of protein recommended for most people. These two different recommendations for protein intake don't yield the same amounts. Although the 2010 Dietary Guidelines limit the intake of saturated and trans fats, Somers places no limit on fat intake as long as you choose the healthy fats she recommends. However, her list of "healthy fats" includes butter, cream, and other full-fat dairy foods that are high in saturated fat. She claims your body will not allow you to overeat these fats because—unlike refined carbohydrates—they send a signal to your body that you are not hungry.

The plan has three phases: Detox phase, during which you release your toxic burden and "blast off pounds," lasts 30 days. It allows 3 servings of carbohydrate foods (approximately 40 to 45 grams) per day (compared to 45 to 60 grams of carbohydrates *per meal* in an average eating plan) in addition to protein and healthy fats. Carbohydrate foods cannot be combined with any fats during this phase.

The Weight-loss Phase allows you to eat up to 4 servings of approved carbohydrate foods a day (approximately 50 to 60 grams). You may add carbohydrate foods to certain meals that contain protein and healthy fats and vegetables. You remain in this phase until you reach your goal weight.

The Lifestyle Phase allows you to eat the good carbohydrates listed in the book "at your discretion." Somers gives several lists of foods to eat and those to avoid during all phases of her plan. She also lists food ingredients you should avoid to reduce your toxic burden.

unique features

Somers' emphasis on environmental toxins and food combining makes her plan different from most low-carb diets. Her method for categorizing acceptable foods is also unique and somewhat confusing. For example, she lists butter, cream, and full-fat cream cheese and sour cream as "Healthy Fats," but lists nonfat varieties of cottage cheese, milk, yogurt, and ricotta cheese simply as approved, not healthy, carbohydrates. This contradicts most nutritional guidelines, which consider full-fat products as less healthy than nonfat versions.

Carbohydrate, protein, and fat allowances

- Carbohydrates: 3 servings per day (approximately 40–45 grams) in the detox phase; 4 servings per day (approximately 50–60 grams) in Level 1.
- Protein: Varies from 90 to 165 grams per day for the average dieter.
- Fat: There are no set allowances for fat as long as approved healthy fats are eaten.

the zone

About the author

Barry Sears, Ph.D., is a former research scientist at Boston University and the Massachusetts Institute of Technology, where he studied the role of lipids (fats) in the body. In 1995, he published *The Zone*, which was number-one on *The New York Times* best-seller list. His latest book, published in 2008, is *Toxic Fat: When Good Fat Turns Bad.* He is the president of the nonprofit Inflammation Research Foundation in Marblehead, MA.

the basic idea

Barry Sears says the "Zone" is a metabolic state in which your body and mind function at their best. This state is achievable with the Zone diet he developed. When you're in the Zone, you are relaxed yet alert and focused. Your body is strong and energetic, and it's working at peak efficiency at all times. According to Sears, being in the Zone slows the aging process; keeps colds and flu at bay; and helps ward off chronic conditions, including heart disease and cancer. Once you're in the Zone, you are able to tap into a virtually unlimited source of energy—your own body fat.

The reason we're not in the Zone is that we eat the wrong foods, says Sears, who maintains that many components of our current diet activate an inflammatory response (what he calls "silent inflammation") that leads to obesity, heart disease, and other diseases. Sears says humans are not genetically geared to eat the amount of carbohydrate they typically take in. He contends that our digestive system was designed to process lean protein and natural carbohydrates such as those found in fruits and fiber-rich vegetables. Eating too many carbohydrates causes insulin levels to rise and leads to an abnormal release of inflammatory hormones that encourage fat storage and contribute to chronic diseases like diabetes and heart disease. Sears believes that food is much more than a fuel supply. He calls food the most powerful drug you'll ever take, because it affects hundreds of hormones that influence your weight and health. According to Sears, the Zone is a real physiological state in which hormones that control silent inflammation are balanced.

how the plan works

Sears promotes a "beneficial" relationship (ratio) between protein and carbohydrate as part of a diet that is, by current recommendations, high in protein and modestly restricted in carbohydrate and fat content. He believes that a diet comprised of 40 percent carbohydrates, 30 percent protein, and 30 percent fat (40/30/30), is the key to controlling insulin production and silent inflammation. That ratio also makes it possible for you to burn excess body fat. The modest amount of carbohydrate in the Zone diet allows the liver to maintain adequate glycogen stores and helps you to avoid ketosis.

Each meal and snack that you eat should contain the beneficial ratios of carbohydrate, protein, and fat. While the Zone isn't a low-fat diet per se, it encourages lean protein choices, and it avoids most grain products, starchy vegetables, and certain types of fruit. Carbohydrate choices should be high in fiber and low on the glycemic index.

Before you jump right into the diet, you must do a bit of math. The first step is to determine your personal protein allowance based on your current weight, percent of body fat, and level of physical activity. (Sears provides detailed instructions for this.) Once you know how much you need, you can figure your carbohydrate and fat allowances. There is no need to count calories or grams of fat, protein, or carbohydrate. Sears has bundled foods into Macronutrient Blocks with predetermined portion sizes, so you do need to weigh and measure foods.

unique features

Sears has determined what he believes is the optimum ratio of carbohydrate, protein, and fat in the diet. Using his macronutrient blocks as a guide, you can always eat the proper ratio. Timing is also important to Sears. You shouldn't let more than five hours elapse without eating a Zone-balanced meal or snack.

Carbohydrate, protein, and fat allowances

- Carbohydrate accounts for 40 percent of calories on the Zone diet.
- Protein needs are unique and must be calculated by the individual, but for most dieters, they generally amount to 30 percent of calories consumed.
- About 30 percent of calories come from fat, with emphasis on omega-3 unsaturated fats.

Meal plan/ recipes

- Contains some suggestions for meal planning and a chapter of low-carb recipes.

diets at a glance

Diet	Main features	Carb allowance	Protein and fat allowances	Ketogenic?	Flexibility rating
The Carbohydrate Addict's Diet	Believes addiction to carbohydrates is a biological disorder. Allows 1 unrestricted meal and 2 low-carb meals/day	None specified; varies based on symptoms	None specified	No	3
The New Atkins for a New You	The lowest of the low-carb diets; high in fat and protein	20 grams Net Carbs/day initially; up to 120 grams for maintenance, less if you gain weight	No set allowances	Yes	3
The New Sugar Busters!	Eliminates refined starch and sugar and promotes lean protein foods and healthy fats.	No set amount, but averages 40% of daily calories	No set amount, but averages 30% of daily calories for each	No	4
The Paleo Diet	Advocates a return to meat-based, Stone-Age diet; discourages foods such as grains that utilize technology	None specified; grains, legumes and dairy products prohibited	None specified	Can be at most restrictive level although not advocated	2

Diet	Main features	Carb allowance	Protein and fat allowances	Ketogenic?	Flexibility rating
The Protein Power LifePlan	Complex plan that can be difficult to use; delves into relationship between diet and disease	Less than 40 grams at the Intervention level; successive levels allow more	Protein varies with weight and height; fat based on weight-loss or maintenance goals	Yes	2
The Schwarzbein Principle II	Goal is to heal metabolism by reducing carbs, exercising, and making other lifestyle changes	Varies, depending on body composition, weight, and activity level	At least 60 grams protein for women and 70 for men daily; no fat allowance	No	3
The South Beach Diet Supercharged	Normalize hormones so you can metabolize carbs; emphasizes eating "Real" organic carbs dense and healthy fats	None specified; emphasizes carbs that can be grown, picked, or harvested	None specified	No	4
Suzanne Somers' Sexy Forever	Avoids various food "toxins"; provides somewhat complicated lists of approved foods	None specified	None specified	No	4
The Zone	Moderate approach to low-carb eating that promotes a beneficial ratio of carb to protein for each meal and snack	40% of daily calories	30% of daily calories for each	No	4

personalize your low-carb plan

Make low-carb work for you. You've learned the fundamentals of low-carb dieting. And you've read the reviews of popular low-carb plans. Now it's time to get personal. Whether you're going to follow one of the reviewed diet plans or you want to create your own, you have to find ways to put the principles of low-carb living to work in your life, to make food and exercise choices that are in keeping with those principles but that also take your goals, your tastes, your lifestyle, and your health into account. You'll find what you need to do just that in this section. Consider it your personal low-carb tool kit, one that you can reach into time and again to ensure that your low-carb dieting efforts are moving you toward your weight-loss goals.

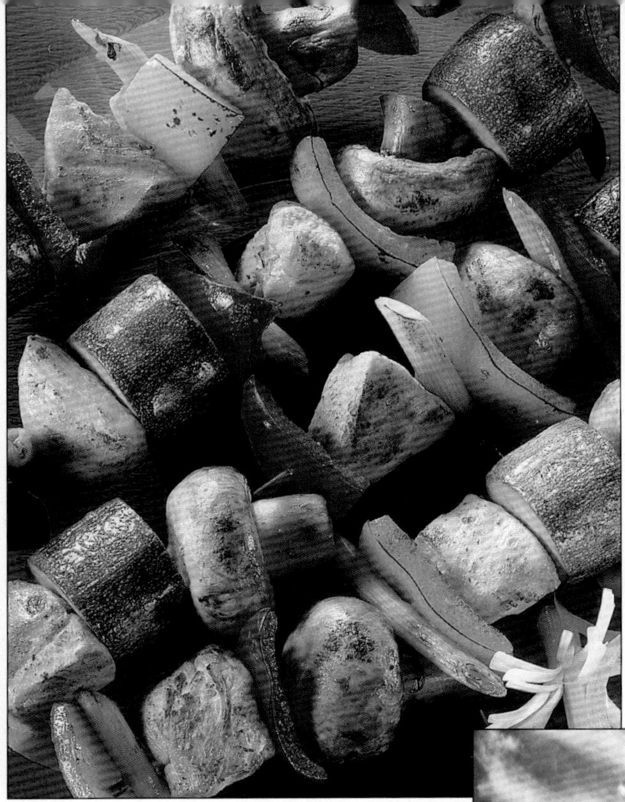

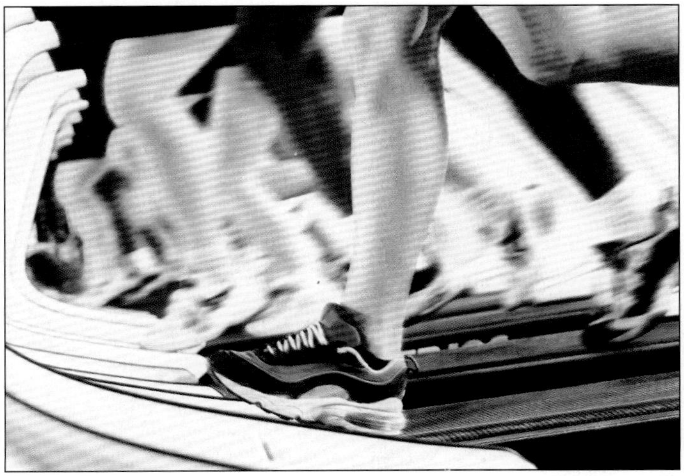

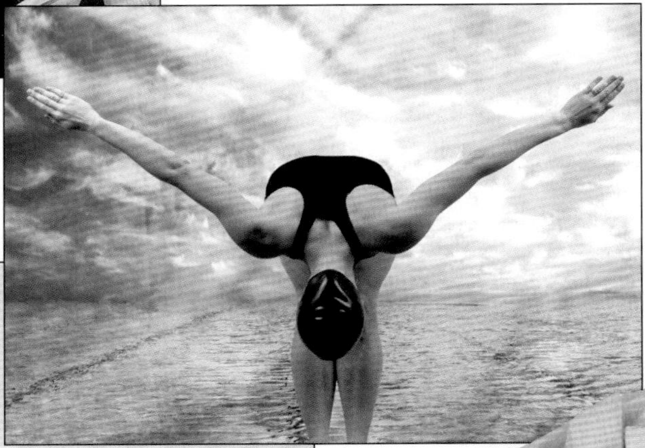

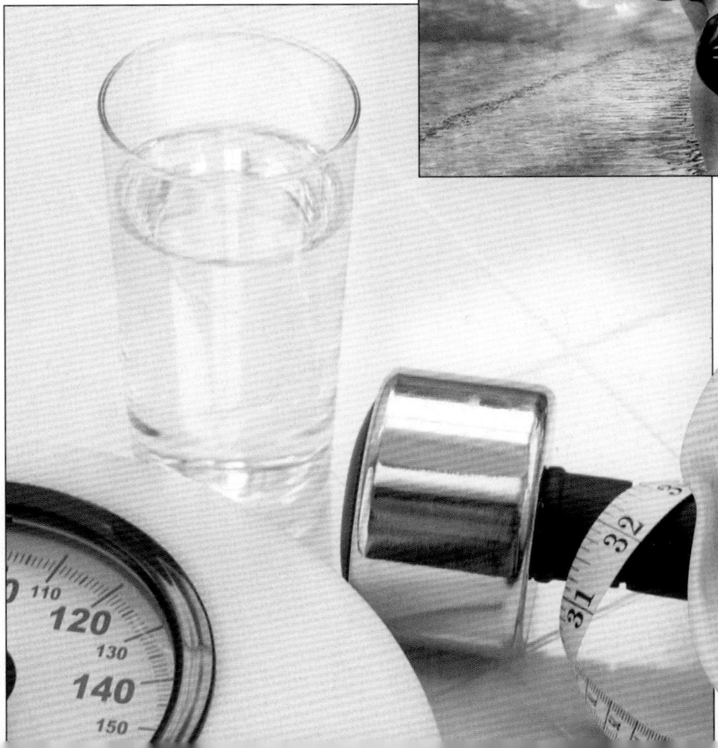
110
120
130
140
150
32
31

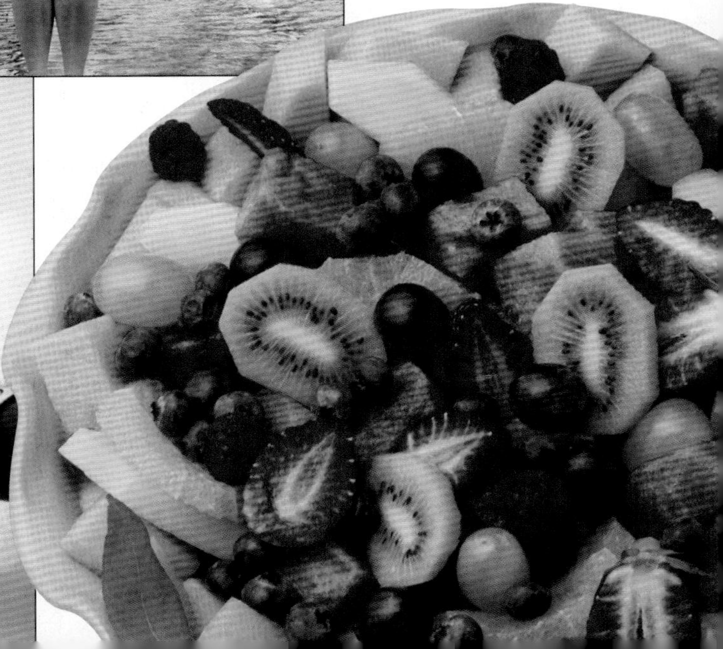

how to build your own low-carb diet

While the medical community has been slow to come around to low-carb eating, it's hard to argue with the benefits of the more moderate low-carb programs, such as the Zone and Sugar Busters!, that don't jeopardize your health for the sake of dropping a dress size. If the rationale and the evidence for low-carb dieting have convinced you to cut carbs, the challenge confronting you now is how to go about it. Do you want to follow one of the low-carb diet plans reviewed earlier or do you prefer a do-it-yourself approach?

tools for low-carb living

When you looked over the diet plans reviewed earlier, did any of them appeal to you? Or did some seem too restrictive while others require too much time and effort to figure out? Perhaps one plan seemed too good to be true while another doesn't eliminate enough carbs for you to lose weight.

If you didn't find just the right plan or a formalized approach feels too constricting, you still can adopt a low-carb lifestyle. All you need are the right tools. In this section, we give you those tools so you can fashion a personalized weight-control plan that works by combining conventional wisdom (you must cut calories to lose weight) with low-carb eating.

getting started: write it down!

You can't make real changes to your diet if you're not conscious of what you eat. Once you know what's going in your mouth every day, you can make dietary changes that will produce weight loss.

The best way to raise your consciousness is to keep track of the foods you eat with a food diary. Why log every morsel? Because it's easy to believe that you avoid simple sugars (carbs), such as table sugar, corn syrup, and fructose, when in reality your diet may be full of these expendable carbohydrates. Food diaries help you to spot sugar sources on food labels and to record the carbohydrate content of processed foods.

Keeping track of what you eat also helps you monitor how much you eat, which influences carbohydrate intake. Portion sizes have grown so large in America today that most of us don't have a clue about what a single serving is supposed to look like. According to MyPyramid, the USDA's food pyramid, a single serving of pasta, for instance, is a half cup. A single serving according to the Nutrition Facts label is one cup. But what you're likely to eat, or what you're likely to be served in a restaurant, is a two-cup portion—four times the single serving allotment on the Pyramid and double the single serving size on the Nutrition Facts panel. The more you keep track of portion sizes, the less likely you'll be to overeat and thwart your weight-loss attempts. Try to weigh and measure foods for at least a few days to get accustomed to correct amounts and sizes. After that, you should be able to accurately eyeball foods and estimate the serving size. For more on portion sizes, please see pages 70–71.

Since emotions often play a role in when, where, and how much food you eat, use your journal to keep track of your mood when you eat as well as where you happen to be (in front of the television, standing at the kitchen counter). Also rate how hungry you are on a scale of 1–5, with 1 being the lowest score. All this information will help you understand how your emotional state affects your eating habits.

Purchase a sturdy notebook that fits in your pocketbook or briefcase. You'll need to bring your food log with you to ensure accurate accounting. Trying to recall what you ate hours later may lead to faulty reporting, especially when you conveniently forget snatching a few of your child's french fries or popping a few pieces of candy in your mouth while driving. After a few days of diligent observance, look for patterns in your eating behaviors. Use food labels and the counter on pages 75–103 to tally your daily intake of carbohydrate grams. Aim for 100 to

Still not losing?

You've curbed carbs, but you've yet to shed a pound. What gives? Here are some reasons why you may not be losing weight.

- **Medications:** Some medications work against weight loss, including insulin and steroids such as prednisone. Check with your physician and pharmacist to establish a link between medicines you take on a regular basis and your weight.

- **Nibbling:** Dieters often underestimate their nibbling, which can amount to hundreds of calories every day. To prevent noshing during meal preparation—or any other time of the day—sip water, chew gum, or nibble on low-carb vegetables such as celery. You can also brush your teeth when tempted to nibble; the minty-fresh flavor of the toothpaste makes food taste bad.

- **Large portion sizes:** Whenever you're baffled by what the scale says, record what you eat for a few days to discover problem areas. Weigh and measure foods to track portion sizes.

- **Exercise:** Relying on diet alone to shed pounds takes longer and reduces your chance of keeping the weight off for good. Consider walking more. Already exercising? Change your routine around. Weight training preserves and builds muscle tissue, which is your body's main calorie-burning tissue.

150 carb grams a day for a lower-carb diet.

label reading: in search of sugar

You have to be a bit of a detective to discover hidden sources of carbohydrate. But you don't need an advanced degree or special skills to uncover them. Most of the time, the information is right under your nose on the Nutrition Facts panel or the ingredient list of any food product.

the nutrition facts panel

The Nutrition Facts panel takes the guesswork out of the carbohydrate content of any packaged food you buy. It lists the total carbohydrate content as well as the amount of dietary fiber and sugars in a single serving. If you're interested in calories, you'll find a listing for them, too.

The listing for grams of total carbohydrate and fiber are the most valuable figures for carbohydrate-counters because they help you fit foods into your daily carbohydrate allowance. Foods that are higher in fiber are also lower on the glycemic-index scale, so they make excellent choices. Aim for at least 25 grams of fiber every day.

A word of caution about the Nutrition Facts panel: It's possible to think that milk, plain yogurt, and cheese contain added sugar and that they are unhealthy because they lack fiber. But neither is the case. Lactose, the naturally occuring carbohydrate in milk, is listed as sugar on food labels even though it's not an added sugar. And dairy products are naturally fiber free. That's because only plant foods provide fiber. But that doesn't make dairy products unhealthy. They're very important sources of protein, bone-building calcium, and vitamin D.

a carbohydrate by any name

There are so many names for sugar, it's important to familiarize yourself with all of them or you could end up unwittingly eating a high-carb diet even as you're trying to cut back. You probably know *sucrose* is a stand-in for *sugar*. It's the white stuff you add to coffee and baked goods. But processed foods, including croutons, spaghetti sauce, and salad dressing, pack a variety of added sugars. Sugar goes by many names in the ingredient list, including:

- Brown sugar
- Cane sugar
- Confectioners' sugar
- Corn syrup and high-fructose corn syrup

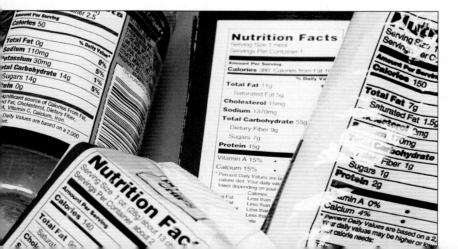

- Crystallized cane sugar or juice
- Date sugar
- Dextrose and dextrin
- Distilled or concentrated fruit sugars
- Fructose
- Glucose and glucose polymers
- Honey
- Invert sugar
- Malt
- Maltose
- Maple syrup
- Molasses
- Raw sugar
- Turbinado sugar

day by day: foods to include

One of the problems with many low-carb regimens is that they recommend limiting or avoiding entire food groups, which can result in nutrient deficiencies that affect your health. No matter what controlled-carbohydrate strategy you choose, here's what you need to include in your daily diet and why.

- 2–3 servings low-fat dairy daily
  Provides protein, bone-building calcium, and vitamin D, all nutrients that reduce your risk for osteoporosis. Dairy foods may also help control blood pressure and help with weight loss.
- 2–3 servings whole grains daily
  Provides fiber that is filling plus B-vitamins, antioxidant vitamins (such as vitamin E), and minerals (such as selenium) that enhance heart health. Three servings a day have been shown to help with weight management.

Committing to low-carb living: good for the entire family

Cutting carbs can benefit every family member, as long as their diets are balanced and age-appropriate. Scaling back on sweets provides the most obvious benefits to everyone. Children may clamor for treats, but they do not need the sugar found in ice cream, cookies, cake, and certain breakfast cereals.

There's no need to go to extremes with kids, however. In fact, keeping bread, potatoes, and cereal off your children's menu may be detrimental to their health because they need carbohydrates for energy. A growing child (excluding infants) requires at least half of his calories from carbohydrate. Offering little ones healthy foods such as meat, poultry, and seafood; whole grains; dairy products; and fruits and vegetables every day while limiting sugary cereals, desserts, and other sweet foods as special treats will give your child the right idea about healthy eating.

- Daily multivitamin supplement
  Acts as a nutritional safety net, filling in any gaps.
- 2–3 servings of fish a week
  To reduce the risk of heart disease.
- Three meals a day
  To keep blood sugars even and reduce feelings of hunger and deprivation that can lead to binges.
- 1–2 cups of whole fruit daily
  To include fiber that promotes a feeling of fullness and antioxidant vitamins and minerals that help fight chronic conditions, including heart disease and cancer.

the fat conundrum

The major problem with fat is that it packs a lot of calories into very small servings, so you may end up eating more than you need. But some low-carb diets advocate shedding your fear of dietary fat to drop pounds. They argue that dietary fat does not promote weight gain because fat cannot provoke the insulin release that stores it. Therefore if you abide by certain low-carb regimens, you may be eating far more fat than you have on other weight-loss programs.

In reality, fat contains more than double the calories of protein or carbohydrate (nine versus four). So how do you explain the success of high-fat eating plans such as the Atkins' diet? Skeptics argue that after a short time of being allowed to gorge on steak, cheese, and cream, dieters tire of these foods and decrease their consumption, dropping their calorie intake to levels that promote weight loss.

Regardless of its role in weight gain and weight loss, we need to remember that fat is essential to good health. Fat

supplies essential fatty acids, the building blocks of important bodily substances that maintain life and promote health. And fat is necessary for transporting and storing vitamins A, D, E, and K.

Not all fat is created equal, however. In the past, all fat in the diet was perceived as bad news for health. But a growing body of evidence suggests that diets rich in unsaturated fats actually protect against heart disease and may help control blood glucose concentrations and elevated triglyceride levels. The 2010 U.S. Dietary Guidelines for Americans encourages consumers to replace saturated and trans fats, found in foods such as meat, cream, cheese, and certain processed foods, with mono- and poly-unsaturated fats, found in foods including nuts, avocados, and vegetable oils. When building your low-carb diet, aim to get 50 to 60 grams of fat a day, the majority of it from monounsaturated and polyunsaturated fat.

fill up on fiber

Dietary fiber, also known as roughage and bulk, is a complex carbohydrate found in fruits, vegetables, legumes, nuts, and whole grains that cannot be broken down by your body during digestion. If your body cannot process it, why is fiber so important to your health? Fiber aids digestion and helps prevent constipation and hemorrhoids. Dietary fiber from whole foods also

protects against obesity, cardiovascular disease, and type 2 diabetes. When whittling your waistline is the goal, fiber is particularly helpful because it promotes a feeling of fullness. Plus, fiber's capacity to provide bulk in your stomach makes it difficult to overeat fiber-rich foods, as compared to low-fiber, highly refined alternatives. For example, it's a lot easier and quicker to drink 8 ounces of apple juice, which is refined and low in fiber, than it is to eat two whole apples, although the juice and the apples have an equivalent number of calories.

Foods high in fiber—carbohydrates your body does not absorb—are good choices for low-carb living. In fact, many low-carb diet proponents recommend choosing foods rich in fiber, including whole grains and certain fruits and vegetables, because fiber slows down the release of glucose into the bloodstream and prevents insulin surges that may interfere with weight loss. Fiber-filled foods are also rich in several vital nutrients, including vitamins, minerals, and phytonutrients—plant substances that guard against heart disease and cancer.

low-carb eating in the real world

It's easier to prepare and eat lower-carb meals in the comfort of your own kitchen, where you know the ingredients involved and have the ability to measure portions. It's much harder to negotiate a low-carb diet when you leave home. Tempting food is absolutely everywhere, whether you're at the movie theater, the ball game, the grocery store, the gas station, or the mall.

The first rule of thumb: Don't let yourself get so hungry that you'll eat anything. Before going out, eat a high-protein snack, and drink a large glass of water to tide you over until your next meal.

When dining out, ask for a doggy bag immediately and put a portion of your meal into it. Ask the wait staff to remove the bread or chip basket from your table, and order extra low-carb vegetables in lieu of potato dishes and rice. Split one dessert among four or more people.

When invited to potluck parties, bring a low-carb dish and fill up on it. It's okay to indulge at times, but curb your carbohydrate consumption to compensate for splurges and avoid "trigger" foods that could cause you to overeat for days.

sample lower carb menu

What does a day's worth of low-carb eating look like? Here's a sample menu to give you a sense of it.

BREAKFAST

   ½ cup whole-grain cereal

   4 ounces 1% low-fat milk

   ½ cup sliced strawberries

SNACK
1 hard-boiled egg
1 cheese stick (1 ounce reduced-fat mozzarella)

LUNCH
Salad (made of: 2 cups mixed salad greens
1 small tomato, chopped
6½ ounce can white tuna, drained
1 tablespoon each: balsamic vinegar and olive oil)
1 ounce whole grain crackers

SNACK
1 ounce almonds

DINNER
Orange Chicken (4-ounce serving boneless, skinless breast served with sauteed chopped onions (¼ cup) and sliced mushrooms (½ cup), browned with small amount of soy sauce and water and ½ tablespoon orange marmalade)
1 cup steamed broccoli
1 teaspoon butter or margarine

SNACK
Fruit Smoothie
(½ cup frozen berries
8 ounces low-fat plain yogurt)
Combine ½ cup frozen berries with 1 teaspoon vanilla extract, 2 ice cubes, 8 ounces low-fat plain yogurt, and artificial sweetener to taste in blender and whip until frothy.

what can I have instead?
Boredom and feelings of deprivation can be the end of any well-intentioned eating plan, low-carb or not. By choosing a lower-carb lifestyle, there is little doubt that you will be doing without some of your favorite foods. However, there is no need to sacrifice all in the name of good health. Eating smaller portions of pasta, rice, bread, and potatoes curbs carbohydrate consumption without denying you them altogether. And taking a new approach to high-carb favorites helps, too. On the next page are some suggestions to start you on the low-carb substitution path.

busting low-carb myths

Some statements about low-carb dieting have been repeated so often that they have taken on mythic proportions. Let's dispel these myths before they hamper your weight-loss efforts.

Myth: Americans have been following the high-carbohydrate, low-fat advice doled out by nutrition professionals, and we are heavier than ever. Clearly, a low-fat diet doesn't work.

Reality: The latest evidence on how we really eat shows that Americans do not follow current dietary recommendations, which specify healthful serving sizes and number of daily portions. Statistics show that most Americans overconsume solid fats, added sugars, refined grains, and sodium (not just carbohydrates). And we don't get enough physical activity to burn off the extra calories. As a result, the obesity rate in America—especially among children—continues to skyrocket.

Myth: Low-carb diets work because they are low in carbohydrates.

Reality: Low-carb proponents argue that carbohydrates promote fat storage, so curbing their intake whittles your waistline. However, for most people, curbing carbohydrates means cutting calories. Each gram of carbohydrate contains four calories, so fewer carbs means a lower calorie intake and weight loss as long as you don't increase calories from other sources. For example, a coffee-lover who drinks 3 cups of java a day and uses 1 tablespoon of sugar in each cup adds 135 calories to the day's intake. Eliminating that sugar amounts to an annual calorie deficit of nearly 47,000 calories, the equivalent of more than 13 pounds of body fat.

Myth: It's possible to eat primarily foods such as steak, eggs, butter, and cream and maintain good health.

Reality: Excess intake of animal foods fills your body with saturated fat and cholesterol, contributing to inflammation that can clog arteries. When arteries that feed the heart become blocked, a heart attack occurs. When there is a clogged artery in the brain, a stroke happens. Beneficial nutrients that stave off heart disease and stroke may be missing in a fat-based diet, making matters worse. Fruits and vegetables are packed with antioxidant vitamins and minerals that can ward off the inflammation that leads to heart disease and type 2 diabetes. Whole grains provide folic acid, a B vitamin linked to a lower risk of heart disease and stroke.

Instead of:	Try:
Pasta with marinara sauce	Whole-wheat pasta or steamed spaghetti squash sautéed with olive oil and garlic and topped with chopped fresh tomatoes
Rice CHEX	Whole-Wheat CHEX
Flavored instant oatmeal	Old-fashioned or quick-cooking oats with added cinnamon
White potatoes, french fries	Baked or roasted sweet potato
Fruit yogurt	Plain, "light," or Greek-style yogurt and ½ cup fresh fruit
Chips	Mixed nuts
Hamburger	Open-faced (whole grain bun) burger made with lean meat with 1 ounce reduced-fat cheese, lettuce, tomato slices, onions
Tuna salad sandwich	Tuna salad on bed of mixed greens plus one serving whole-grain crackers
Peanut butter	Natural peanut butter with no added sugar or salt
Pepperoni pizza	1 slice vegetable pizza on whole-wheat crust
Milk chocolate bar	Strawberries dipped in melted dark chocolate
Ice cream frappé	Smoothie prepared with ½ cup plain or Greek yogurt, ½ cup berries, ice cubes, and vanilla extract
Orange juice	Whole orange
Mixed cocktail	4 ounces red or white wine
Plain bagel	2 slices "light" whole-grain bread
Bottled Italian dressing	Balsamic vinegar and oil

exercise: the universal fitness tool

When it comes to the battle of the bulge, no matter what type of diet you follow, there's no more universally helpful weight-loss tool than exercise. Making exercise a regular habit and learning to incorporate more activity into your day can make any diet more powerful. Paired with c low-carb diet, regular physical activity can help you burn more fat and reach your goals sooner. Keep it up even after you've lost the pounds, and exercise will help you maintain that weight loss.

the best exercise

Any form of exercise will help you burn extra calories and, therefore, help you control your weight. Aerobic exercises, such as walking, running, swimming, or cycling, are especially good fat burners. For an exercise to be considered aerobic, it must work the large muscles—such as those in the legs and buttocks or arms and shoulders—continuously for an extended period of time. In so doing, it increases your body's demand for oxygen, forcing your breathing and heart rate to speed up. And that's exactly what you want when you're trying to lose weight, because your body needs that extra oxygen in order to release stored body fat and use it as fuel for your working muscles. The longer you keep up the activity, the more stored body fat is released and burned as fuel.

What's the best aerobic exercise for *you* to do? Only you know the answer. Choose the one you are most likely to enjoy and stick with for the duration—not just during weight loss but for the rest of your life. Legions of dieters who have lost weight and managed to keep it off over the years say that exercise is the key. But an exercise that is too difficult to master, can only be done when the weather cooperates or during certain times of the year, or that you simply don't like doing, is one that won't be very effective in the long run.

Let's face it, we all know that even when we have the best intentions, it's

easy to find an excuse not to exercise. So why choose an activity that has a lot of requirements and, as a result, a lot of ready-made excuses built in? Better to find something that you can do alone or with someone else, in good weather and bad, without having to drive across town, buy loads of equipment, or block out hours of every day.

That's why, at least at the beginning, as you learn how to make exercising a habit that you actually look forward to, we suggest something as simple and versatile as walking. Almost everybody can do it. It doesn't require a big investment in equipment. It can be done outdoors, in the city, suburbs, or rural areas. It can be done indoors, either in a shopping mall or a community center, in a gym, or even at home on a treadmill. It can be done alone, with a friend, or with other regular walkers. It can be done in one chunk or, when your schedule is tight, in smaller increments. It can even be done when you're

on vacation or traveling for business.

To that end, we've included a walking program that you can adjust to your current level of fitness. It can provide you with structure and suggestions to get you started toward that trimmer body you desire.

maybe you need a little spice?

What if walking just isn't your style or you're looking to add more excitement or challenge to your exercise routine? Well, they do say that variety is the spice of life. And if you prefer to vary the activities you do to keep exercise enjoyable, go for it. Try jogging, swimming, cycling, an aerobics class, or an exercise video. Take a country or salsa dancing class, join a recreational volleyball league, or go to your local park and play some pickup basketball. As long as the exercise gets your heart pumping harder, your breath coming quicker, and your muscles moving, it can be a part of your exercise plan— especially if it keeps you committed. If you're a tennis fan, you could schedule a tennis match with a friend twice a week, then walk (or cycle or jog) on other days or when your partner cancels at the last minute. The key is to always have a backup activity for the days or weeks that your preferred

Taking your pulse

When you're exercising, give yourself time to raise your heart rate. Then check your pulse during the routine to see if you're in your target zone.

To check your pulse, place the index and middle finger of one hand on the underside of the wrist of your other hand. You should be able to feel your pulse just below the heel of your hand. (If you don't feel your pulse right away, slide your fingers around the wrist area until you can feel the beats.) Count the beats for 15 seconds. Then multiply that number by four to get the beats per minute. Try to take your pulse while continuing to perform the exercise if possible, or take it as quickly as possible so your heart rate doesn't have a chance to fall.

If your pulse during exercise falls below your target zone, you'll need to exercise a little harder. If your pulse is above your target zone, ease up on the intensity. After some practice, you may even find that you can tell if you're working in your target zone based just on how hard you feel you're working. Even so, it doesn't hurt to check your pulse from time to time to be sure.

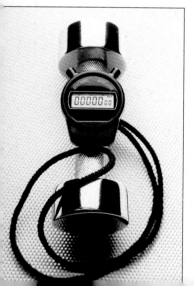

exercise appointments fall through. This way, you'll be less likely to skip the exercise and just plop yourself on the couch in front of the television, with a bag of chips and soda in hand.

the one-two punch against pounds

Wouldn't it be great if you could burn extra calories when you're lying around watching television or surfing on your computer? Well, as miraculous as it may seem, you really can. The way to do it is to add a little strength training to your regular exercise routine.

Strength training—whether it's by lifting free weights, pulling against resistance bands (those things that look like giant rubber bands), using weight or resistance machines, or even doing good ol' push-ups and sit-ups—builds muscle. By building more muscle tissue, you increase your metabolism. That's because muscle is very active tissue, while fat is not. The more muscle you have, the more calories you burn, even when you're lounging on the sofa or sitting at your desk. So, if you do two or three strength-building sessions a week, you really can burn more calories (and thus, more body fat) during those times when your body isn't in motion. Indeed, one study found that women who built muscle by strength training twice a week burned up to 300 more calories a day.

how much is enough?

Forget the "no pain, no gain" theory of exercise. Moderation is the key. Here's what you need to know:

frequency: Exercising aerobically three times a week is the minimum. If you're really serious about losing body fat, however, shoot for five times a week or even every day. Build up to that frequency gradually, though, especially if you've been relatively inactive lately. You should also engage in at least two strength-training sessions each week. Schedule your strength training for alternate days. This way, your muscles get their needed recovery time between workouts—time your muscles need to repair and build them-selves up. Or, if you would like to do some strength training every day, alternate the muscle groups that you work. For instance, you might do leg and lower back work on Monday, do arm and chest exercises on Tuesday, then go back to the leg and back exercises on Wednesday.

intensity: If your chosen exercise makes your heart beat a little faster and you even "break a sweat," the intensity of your exercise is probably about right. You should be able to carry on a conversation while you exercise, but if you can easily belt out a tune, you need to pick up the pace a bit.

A more precise way to measure intensity is by monitoring your heart rate during exercise. You'll get the best results by working in what's called your "target heart-rate zone." Your target zone is 50 to 85 percent of your maximum heart rate per minute. Your maximum heart rate can be determined through a stress test given by your physician. But if you're in good health, you can get a reasonably accurate idea of your maximum heart rate by subtracting your age from 220. Once you know your maximum heart rate, multiply it by 0.50 and 0.85 to find the lower and upper ends of your target zone respectively. (You'll find an example of how to calculate your target zone in the box on page 51.) Then, as you exercise, check your pulse (see the box on the opposite page) occasionally to be sure that you are working in

your target zone.

time: Twenty minutes in your target zone is the minimum, but 30 minutes is a good goal for most people. Of course, if you can stretch that to 40, 50, or even 60 minutes a day, you'll burn even more body fat. Again, though, if you have been sedentary, start with shorter workouts and increase the time gradually.

If you have a week when you are extremely busy, instead of just skipping exercise altogether, break your 30 minutes a day into two or three shorter workouts. For instance, you might ride an exercise bike for 10 to 15 minutes before work, then get an additional 10 to 15 minutes of walking in during your lunch hour or after dinner. Try to make these shorter sessions more intense by working at the higher end of your target heart-rate zone if you can. You may not get the same fat-burning effect as you would by exercising continuously for 30 or 40 minutes, but you will burn some calories and, more importantly, you'll keep up your exercise habit. Aim for consistency. Your body reaps rewards whenever you get up and get moving.

Fat-burning tip

A moderate pace allows you to exercise longer than a more intense one. But if you have limited time to exercise, you can burn more body fat—without burning yourself out—by picking up the pace for one- to three-minute intervals during your workout. For example, try alternating five or ten minutes of moderate effort with three minutes of more-intense effort throughout the exercise session.

commitment: If you truly want to lose weight without lowering your calorie intake to dangerous levels, you must exercise. There's no two ways about it. You must commit yourself to exercising and getting more physical. One way to help yourself fulfill that commitment is to schedule exercise sessions into your day. If you use any type of planner or calendar, mark down the time you will allot to exercise in your weekly schedule. Consider it a commitment like any other. If you have an important meeting or event to attend or a task or errand that must be done, you probably write it down. Your exercise sessions should have the same importance. Scheduling—and keeping—your exercise appointments also helps you feel a sense of accomplishment when you look back over your week and see that you met your exercise goals.

safety check

Most healthy adults can start a sensible exercise program without elaborate medical testing. But if you have any chronic medical problems, are pregnant, or are very overweight, it's best to consult your doctor before beginning a regular exercise program. If you have been inactive for a long time, have never exercised regularly before, or are very overweight, be sure to start out slowly (actually, that's not bad advice for anyone beginning a new exercise routine).

To give your heart and muscles time to adjust, start each aerobic exercise session with a few minutes of slower-paced activity, and end each session with a few minutes at that same slower pace. For example, if you plan to go jogging, spend about five minutes walking or jogging slowly to get warmed up, then jog at your normal pace for 20 minutes or more, and finally, cool down at the end with five more minutes of slow jogging or walking.

And no matter what type of exercise you're doing, if the activity hurts, slow down until it doesn't hurt anymore or just stop the activity. Exercise should be challenging and should make demands on your body, but it should not be painful. Likewise, be sure to move into a new exercise program gradually, no matter what shape you're in. Increase the intensity of the movement or the heaviness of the weight by steps over time. Charging head on into a new activity, without giving your body a chance to work up its tolerance, will set you up for injury. And there's nothing that can put the kibosh on an exercise program, on a weight-loss program, and on your motivation like an injury. So build your exercise routine gradually.

finishing touches

If you really want to lose weight and keep it off for good, your goal should be to get and stay active, not just through regular exercise, but throughout your daily routine. You may wonder how you can, when you barely find the time to exercise as it is. Well, sometimes the solutions to our problems are staring us right in the face and we just don't recognize them. That may very well be the case when it comes to living a more active lifestyle.

To illustrate, think about how many times you've gone to the mall or the grocery store and spent time driving around looking or waiting for that spot by the door. Chances are there were plenty of open spots farther away, but, of course, they seemed *so far.* And you'd *have to walk* all that way. But if you turned that "have to" into "be able to," and spent that same time walking instead of waiting, you'd have burned extra calories and spent no "extra" time at all.

In everyday life, there are plenty of situations in which we spend as much or more time taking the less active—but supposedly more convenient—route, only to complain about the time and inconvenience of having to exercise. If we just start looking at those situations as calorie-burning opportunities, chances to get our muscles moving and our blood pumping, living an active life becomes as easy as putting one foot in front of the other.

So to put the finishing touches on your "active" pursuit of weight loss, start tuning in to these seemingly small opportunities to move closer to your weight-

loss goals. Here are some other suggestions:

- Use the stairs instead of the elevator or escalator.
- Get off the bus a stop early and walk the rest of the way.
- Avoid driving distances of less than ½ mile; walk or ride or even roll there on inline skates instead.
- Walk around while you talk on the phone.
- Walk your dog instead of just letting him do his duty in the yard.
- Deliver messages in person instead of calling or sending an e-mail.
- Take a short exercise break instead of a coffee break.
- At work, use the restroom farthest from your desk.
- Ride a stationary bike, walk a treadmill, march in place, or do push-ups while you watch television.
- Wash the car by hand.
- Take a walk instead of lingering over leftovers.
- Bring the groceries from the car into the house one bag at a time.

It's fairly simple to find ways to boost your calorie burning and live a more active life. Soon it will become second nature. And go ahead and give a friendly wave as you walk swiftly and proudly by that poor person still waiting for that closer parking space.

walk off pounds!

These days, all you have to do is a little channel surfing and you'll see a handful of advertisements for products claiming to be the best new thing for weight loss. Take it off; keep it off; trim it down; firm it up; get stronger; improve your looks, personality, and social life in 15 minutes a day. What's a consumer to believe?

While it is virtually impossible to choose one "best" weight-loss activity for everyone, any activity vying for the title would need to be totally adaptable to all fitness levels, convenient, relatively inexpensive, functional in a way that makes us stronger and better prepared for the demands of everyday life, and an outstanding calorie burner.

Walking is one activity that can meet this challenge. Because of its versatility, it has stepped to the forefront of popularity among U.S. exercisers. For most people, a more convenient activity cannot be found. It's easy to adjust walking to your personal fitness level by changing speed, duration, or terrain. It's a weight-bearing activity, so it can help strengthen bones. And, best of all, walking makes it very easy to burn loads of calories.

You can expect to burn 100 to 200 calories during a moderately paced 30-minute walk. By following the program outlined here, you can go from casual walker to power walker and more than double that rate of calorie burning.

If weight loss is your goal, you'll want to burn at least 300 extra calories a day, or about 1,500 extra calories a week. That can lead to half a pound of weight loss a week even if you don't trim calories from your diet. If you also cut just 400 calories from your daily food intake, you could lose five pounds in a month.

go for the (calorie) burn

Engaging in long, slow exercise sessions has been touted as the best way to lose fat, because you burn more fat calories at a low intensity. Research suggests, however, that low-intensity training does not result in faster weight loss. Renowned weight-loss researcher Jack Wilmore, Ph.D., of Texas A&M University, explains, "It is misleading because the lower intensity does burn a higher percentage of fat versus carbohydrate. However, high intensity exercise burns more total calories, and even though the percentage of fat burned is lower, the total fat burned is greater at high intensity." In other words, if you compare an hour's worth of low-intensity exercise to an hour's worth of high-intensity exercise, you'll actually burn more total fat and calories working at the higher intensity. And that can be an important consideration, since many of us have to struggle to find time to exercise.

"The American way is to try to pack more into less time. It makes sense to increase your fitness because you maximize your time by increasing the number of calories you can burn in a workout," says Peggy Norwood Keating, former fitness director at the Duke University Diet and Fitness Center in Durham, North Carolina. By improving your fitness, you can fit more calorie burning into a shorter period of time.

Here's how it works. The number of calories you burn per mile is fairly constant, regardless of whether you walk that distance or run it. It's affected primarily by your own body weight. A 140-pound person burns approximately 80 calories per mile. (To figure out how many calories you burn, add or subtract five calories per mile for

S-t-r-e-t-c-h!

To increase your flexibility and help prevent injury, spend several minutes at the end of your workout stretching the muscles in the following areas (hold each stretch for 20 to 60 seconds):

Ankles: Rotate each ankle through a full range of motion by tracing large circles with your toes, first in a clockwise direction and then counterclockwise.

Shins: Sit down with your legs extended and your heels on the ground, and gently point your toes toward the ground.

Calves: Lean against a wall, with your palms on the wall and your fingers pointing up, and step back with one leg. Keep the back leg straight and gently press the heel into the floor. Switch leg positions and repeat.

Quadriceps (front of thigh): Stand with your right hand on a wall or chair for balance. Bend your left knee and, grasping the left ankle with your left hand, pull your left foot toward your buttocks. Repeat with the opposite leg.

Hamstrings (back of thigh): Lie face up on the floor with your right leg bent, your right foot flat on the floor, and your left leg extended. Grasping the back of your left knee, bend your left knee and pull your left leg toward your chest. Then gently straighten the left knee and push your left heel toward the ceiling. Release and repeat with the right leg.

Lower back: Lie on your back and pull both legs to your chest until your hips lift from the floor. Hold for a count of five. Rock back and forth if that feels good. Then release.

every ten pounds over or under 140.) At 140 pounds, walking 2.5 miles per hour (a mile in 24 minutes), you will burn 100 calories during a 30-minute walk. If you speed up your pace and walk at four miles per hour (a mile in 15 minutes), you will burn 160 calories in the same amount of time. Add short intervals of running within that half hour, and the number of calories you burn could top 300, because you will end up covering more miles in the same amount of time.

for the health of it

The benefits of a walking routine go beyond weight loss to improvements in physical health and mental attitude. And the more active you become, the more benefits you gain. (There is a qualifier, however: The more you exercise, the greater your risk of injury or burn-out. So as with any habit, use common sense and don't go overboard.)

In general, you can rack up most of the health benefits of physical activity—including controlling blood pressure and blood sugar and decreasing the risk of heart disease—by burning an extra 800 to 1,000 calories a week. You can even improve your health profile by getting a total of 30 minutes of noncontinuous exercise each day—say a ten-minute walk in the morning, a ten-minute walk at lunch, and a ten-minute walk after work. Unlike weight loss, these health benefits are affected more by increasing the *amount* of exercise rather than the *intensity.*

gauging your intensity

Since the number of calories you burn in a specific period of time depends in part on the intensity of your workout, you need to be able to measure how hard your body is working. You'll find instructions for calculating what's called your target heart-rate zone in "Figuring Your Target Zone" on page 51. During your walking workouts, you will want to aim for a training range between 50 and 85 percent of your maximum heart rate; where in that range you work will depend on the level of walking workout you choose. You can also just rely on your own sense of how hard you are working.

sneak up on your training zone

When you begin a walking workout session, you can't just jump right into your training zone. You need to sneak up on that zone with five to ten minutes of easy walking first. By gradually increasing the pace, you slowly bring your effort and heart rate into your training zone. Starting slowly also warms up your muscles, ligaments, and tendons. The result is that your muscles are ready to use more oxygen, you move more easily, and you are less susceptible to injury.

It's important to back out of a workout the same way. At the end of the workout, do another five to ten minutes of easy walking to bring your heart rate back down near your resting level. The movement of the muscles will keep the blood from pooling in your hands and feet, which could lead to light-headedness or fainting. The end of the workout, when your muscles are very warm, is the best time to stretch (see the stretches in the box "S-t-r-e-t-c-h" on page 57).

time to play

It would be impractical to propose one walking program for every schedule, fitness level, and degree of motivation. So this program has three levels. It's not necessary to "graduate" from one level to the next if you are satisfied with the calorie burning and fitness results you are already getting from the level that you are on. On the other hand, you might find that stepping up your intensity helps keep you challenged or gives you the boost you need to get over a weight-loss plateau, when the pounds don't seem to be budging.

level I—lifestyle walking

This program is for beginning exercisers who want the tremendous health

Form is everything

Practice these posture pointers as you walk:
- Keep your body stacked like a column, with your ears, shoulders, hips, knees, and ankles aligned directly over one another.
- Hold your pelvis in a position that maintains the natural curve in your lower back without excessive arching (lordosis) or flattening (tucking the buttocks too far underneath you). Try squeezing a towel between the upper thighs to help bring the pelvis into a good position. Then drop the towel but maintain that position. Relax your buttocks, but contract your abdominals lightly to hold your pelvis in this position as you walk.
- To help determine if you are aligning your head over your shoulders, try this exercise: Put your fingers to your lips as if you were smoking a cigarette (make-believe only, please). Leaving your fingers exactly where they are, gently lean your head directly backward until you feel resistance in the neck muscles, then relax forward just until the pressure disappears. The distance between your face and your fingers is how much out of line you typically hold your head.
- Walk tall without leaning forward at the waist. Don't slouch or stare at the ground as you walk; this restricts your breathing.
- Do not overstride. Your stride should be a comfortable length and you should glide without bouncing.
- Push off fully with the rear leg to work the entire leg and the buttocks.

benefits that even 30 minutes of daily activity can bring but are not ready for a more time-consuming workout program. You literally squeeze activity into your life by fitting walking into your day's activities. Aim for at least 30 minutes of moderate- to brisk-paced walking a day. A good place to start is your daily commute. If you can't walk the entire distance, you can walk to the subway or bus stop or get on or off one stop early. Get off the elevator one floor early and take the stairs. Try to avoid escalators or moving sidewalks that you find in airports; they are called

energy savers, but you should start thinking of them as calorie-storage systems.

Once you master these, you can begin getting off of the bus and the elevator two, three, or four stops early. Also, add very short walking breaks during the day. Relax, clear your head, and add five minutes to your daily activity total at the same time.

level II—walking for a workout

This level makes structured exercise a part of your daily routine. The extra time allotted to exercise makes it possible to safely achieve the level of exertion necessary to significantly improve your fitness and burn more calories.

Your first goal is to walk at a comfortable pace for 15 to 20 minutes. Increase the total time of your daily walks by no more than five minutes each week until you reach 30 to 45 minutes per walk.

Next, increase your pace during the training phase of your workout, which is the 20- to 30-minute period between warmup and cooldown. The amount of effort or intensity you put in should be challenging, but you should still be able to hold a conversation while you

exercise. (If you don't have a partner to talk to and aren't afraid to look a little silly, try singing a song, reciting a poem, or going over your daily schedule out loud.) In terms of your heart-rate zone, aim for 60 to 75 percent of your maximum.

level III—interval training

This phase is for walkers who want an extra challenge in their workouts and who want to maximize their calorie-burning potential. The basis of this phase is interval training, which is simply alternating periods of high-intensity work with rest intervals of easy walking.

The benefits include even greater improvement in cardiovascular fitness; extra work for the muscles, which helps make them stronger; and more calories burned per minute. It also provides a challenge, which, for some folks, could be the difference between staying on the exercise bandwagon or falling off.

One possible drawback is an increased chance of injury, and this makes paying attention to proper rest, stretching, and form even more important. In addition, it's advisable that you successfully complete at least six weeks of the Level II workout, with your heart rate in the target zone for at least 20 minutes of each workout session, before attempting the Level III workout.

Many types of activities can be used to increase your workout intensity.

Intervals of very brisk walking may be enough, especially when you first start at this level. But you may also want to try intervals of running, walking stairs, "bench stepping" on an aerobic step, or climbing rolling hills on an outdoor walk. These activities require that you "lift" the body weight more than you do when walking on level ground and can greatly increase the calories burned per mile. During a 60-minute walk, you could potentially increase your calorie burning by 20 percent if you spend five or six intervals climbing a long hill, or hills, with a 9- to 10-percent grade.

Begin your interval program by interspersing three 3- to 5-minute high-intensity intervals ("high intensity" meaning an effort that pushed your heart rate up to about 80 percent of your maximum). This effort should be hard but controlled, and you should not be exhausted at the end of the interval. Recover for an equal amount of time with easy walking.

If you want the variety of interval training but are not yet up to the rigors of the really high intensities, try making the transition more gradually. Increase your effort so that your heart rate is at least 75 percent of your maximum for three to five minutes, and rest for only one minute in between. Your intense intervals won't be quite as strenuous, but the shorter rests will make the overall workout more demanding.

To increase calorie burning even more, decrease the length of the high-intensity interval and increase the length of the rest interval. Sound too easy? Well, the reason you increase the length of the rest interval is so that you can work even harder during the high-intensity intervals. Do one to two minutes at a heart rate of 85 percent, or even a bit more, of your maximum (but never above your maximum). This effort should feel hard to very hard. Then spend twice as much time in your rest interval, walking at an easy pace. In other words, after one minute of working at 85 percent of your maximum, spend two minutes walking at 65 to 70 percent. (Due to the cardiovascular demands of such high-intensity work, it's important to get your doctor's approval before increasing your workout intensity to this level.)

Even after you begin this interval program, don't forget to include walks from Levels I and II in your weekly routine. Lifestyle walking is especially important in keeping you more active, and it actually becomes easier after you have gotten more fit through structured, high-intensity exercise. On days when time is tight and five to ten minutes is all you have, take advantage of it with a short "moving break" to clear your head. It will help reduce stress and keep you on track to prevent that feeling of falling off the exercise bandwagon. Have fun and enjoy being active!

Fat-Burning Tip

To increase your energy expenditure—and the amount of fat that you burn—during workouts, get your upper body in on the act, too. You can increase the calories you burn by as much as 10 percent by pumping your arms vigorously as you walk. Joggers and step-aerobicizers can also boost their calorie burning by adding arm movements. If you use or are thinking of purchasing a stair-climbing machine or stationary bicycle, opt for one with movable handlebars that you pump with your arms.

strengthening exercises to burn more fat

You may have worn holes in the soles of your sneakers from walking, chlorine-bleached your hair from swimming laps, or ridden your bicycle to the point of needing a good tune-up. But if you're doing only aerobic exercise, your exercise program is incomplete. A weight-loss regimen that relies on a low-carb diet and aerobic exercise is like a car that has enough gas and fully inflated wheels but was built with too small an engine.

Your muscles are your body's engine, and developing them through strength training is your way of burning fuel (calories). The more muscles you have and the larger they are, the more fuel you will burn. And that muscular engine will keep burning fuel even when the car is idling at the drive-in movie or parked in the garage for the night.

what's in it for me?

It's easy to overlook the benefits of strength training. After all, you can see how jogging or walking the treadmill can expend lots of calories and help you lose weight. But, though the benefits of strength training aren't as obvious, they are actually even more plentiful.

Building your lean muscle tissue will give you:
- Greater strength in performing everyday activities, such as carrying the groceries
- A higher metabolism, so you burn more calories even at rest
- Stronger bones
- An increased ability to do aerobic exercise
- Better body composition (an improved ratio of lean tissue to fat)
- A more toned and slim-looking physique
- Protection against injury

looking gooood!

Let's talk for a minute about how good you're going to look. After all, that's one of the main reasons you're dieting and exercising, isn't it? And when you get discouraged, isn't it looking better, along with feeling better, that keeps you motivated?

Strength training several times a week will firm you up, so you're going to look slimmer even if you don't lose weight. Although muscle tissue is more dense than fat, meaning it weighs more than fat, it actually takes up about 20 percent less room. As a result, your waistline, your arms, and your legs will shrink as you strengthen those muscles, even if the number on your scale stays the same or even increases a bit. Your clothes will fit differently, and you'll have a leaner look. The change in appearance can be dramatic.

One more thing: Strength training helps the parts of your body that tend to be the most affected by gravity's pull. Those parts will stay firmer, and for longer, as a result of your strength-training efforts. So you can add looking younger to the list of strength-training benefits.

getting started

It can be confusing, but the terms *strength training, weight training, weight lifting,* and *resistance training* all refer to the same thing: exercises that build and tone muscle. When you do a strength-training exercise, your muscle contracts against resistance. That resistance can be the weight of your own body (as when you do sit-ups or push-ups), a hand weight (also called a free weight or dumbbell), a resistance band (a long elastic loop), wrist and/or ankle weights (anchored to wrist or ankle with straps), or a weight machine (either at the gym or at home).

Some other words you need to know before you begin are *repetition* and *set.* A repetition, or *rep,* is the number of times you actually do a particular exercise. A *set* is the amount of times you complete a group of repetitions. For example, if you're to do three sets of push-ups at 12 reps each, you do 12 push-ups, rest, do 12 more, rest, do 12 a third time, and you're done.

general guidelines

Before using any kind of weights, you first need to figure out how much weight to start with. A general guideline is that you should be able to complete at least two sets of at least eight

Don't bulk me up!

Some people, especially women, avoid strength training because they think they'll end up looking like a female bodybuilder. Nothing could be farther from the truth. When you strength train, you'll be building a lean, toned look, not a bulky one.

The truth is, bodybuilders have to work very, very hard to achieve that bulky look, and they do it by working their muscles using very heavy weights lifted through only a few repetitions. The amount of weight is increased as soon as the muscle can withstand it.

You, on the other hand, will do a strength-training routine that involves lighter weights lifted through many repetitions. As your muscles get stronger and gain stamina, more repetitions will be added. Weight is increased very slowly.

Make your own weights

If you don't want to spring for a set of weights, especially when you're just starting out, you can make weights from items you have on hand in the kitchen. Some people like to use soup cans in the beginning. Just weigh them before you start so you know how much weight you're lifting. You also can make own your weights. One method is to pour a pound or more of beans or rice into an old sock and tie it securely. Another is to fill small plastic milk or juice jugs with the amount of beans or rice you want to use.

controlled repetitions with the weight you choose. If you can't, it's too heavy. On the other hand, if you can comfortably do more than three sets of 12 repetitions, it's time to move up to a heavier weight. Also, you may need different weights for different exercises.

It's important to give your muscles a day of rest in between workouts. But that doesn't mean you can't strength train every day if you want to. All you need to do is work the upper body one day and the lower body the next day. If you prefer to skip a day, however, you can strength train your whole body at one session, then take the next day off.

Always exhale as you contract a muscle or lift a weight. Then inhale as you relax the muscle or lower the weight.

Proper form is very important when you're strength training. To avoid injury and to get the most out of your routine, you need to keep your body properly aligned, breathe correctly, and contract and release your muscles slowly and smoothly. It may be worth the expense to hire a personal trainer for one session to get you going safely. A trainer can also design a strength-training program unique to your physique, your abilities, and your lifestyle. Instructors can be found at local YMCAs, community centers, community colleges, athletic clubs, and gyms. If you do go that route, just be sure to check the trainer's

credentials. A certified trainer will be happy to oblige.

a sample workout

If you want to start a strength-training routine but aren't sure what exercises to include, try the ones we describe below. They're basic to any strength-training program.

exercises for the upper body

The following exercises should be performed for two to three sets of 8 to 12 repetitions.

1. **BICEPS CURL** *(tones the biceps)*
   Sit on the edge of a stool or bench or stand with your knees slightly bent, about hip-distance apart. Hold one weight in each hand and extend your arms down the front of your thighs, with the inner forearms facing outward. Without moving the upper arms, slowly lift the weights, for four counts, until they are almost touching your upper arms. At the peak of the movement, flex the biceps muscles and hold for two counts. Slowly lower the weights to the starting position, to the count of four.

2. **TRICEPS KICKBACK** *(tones the back of the upper arms)*
   Stand with your knees bent, feet about hip-distance apart. Lean slightly forward, take a weight in each hand and hold them right next to your hips. Elbows should be bent and held closely to your sides. With-

out moving your upper arms or your elbows, straighten the arms and extend the weights as high as you can in back of you, to the count of four. Flex the triceps and hold for two counts. Slowly lower the weights to the starting position to the count of four.

3. TRICEPS EXTENSION *(tones the back of the upper arms)*
Sit erect in a low-backed chair or on a stool or exercise bench. Hold the weight in your right hand. Raise your right arm straight above your right shoulder.

Keep your elbows pointed up (towards the ceiling) as you slowly lower the weight behind your head. Then slowly press the weight back up to the starting position. Alternate arms after completing each set.

3. SIDE RAISE *(tones the middle deltoid muscle, at the side of the shoulder)*
Hold a weight in each hand, with the arms extended down the sides of the thighs, palms facing inward. Slowly raise your arms out to the side until the weights are shoulder level, to a count of four. Hold for two counts, then slowly lower to the starting position, also to a count of four.

5. CHEST FLY *(tones the pectoralis major muscles)*
Lie on a weight bench, aerobics step (if you have one), or the floor. Hold a weight in each hand, arms

extended out to the sides at chest level, the insides of the forearms facing up toward the ceiling. Your arms should remain rigid throughout the exercise, although the elbows should be slightly bent (not locked). Slowly bring the weights together directly above your chest, to the count of four. Hold for two counts, then slowly lower to the starting position, to the count of four.

exercises for the lower body
The following exercises should be performed for three sets of 8 to 12 repetitions. These exercises can be done

with or without ankle weights. Wearing ankle weights will increase the intensity of the exercises. *Do not perform these exercises to the point of discomfort, and stop doing the exercise if you feel pain.*

1. **OUTER THIGH LIFT** *(tones the outer thigh and gluteal muscles)*
Lie on your side with your head resting on your extended arm. Bend your bottom knee to increase your base of support. Make sure your hips are stacked one above the other and perpendicular to the floor.

Lift your top leg about two feet, with your foot parallel to the ceiling and your toe pointed.

Continue with the training progression that follows, completing all repetitions. Then switch to the other side.

- Complete three sets of 8 repetitions—two counts up, hold for two counts, down in two counts.
- Complete two sets of 8 repetitions—small pulses up, down in one count.
- Complete one set of 8 small pulses.

2. **INNER THIGH LIFT** *(tones and develops the inner thigh)*
Lie on your left side, propping yourself up on your left elbow and forearm. Cross the right leg over the left, placing the right foot on the floor in front of your left knee, right knee pointed toward the ceiling. Check to be sure your left leg is aligned with your hip, waist, and shoulder.

Extend the left leg, with the inner thigh facing the ceiling and the foot flexed. Lift the left leg toward the ceiling. At the peak of the movement, tighten the inner thigh muscle. Lower the leg.

Follow the training progression described below. Don't worry if you can't do the whole routine at first. Simply do as many sets as you can and gradually work up to doing the whole progression.

- Complete three sets of 8 repetitions—two counts up, hold for two counts, down in two counts.

- Complete two sets of 8 repetitions —three small pulses up, down in one count.
- Complete three sets of 8 small pulses

When you've completed all repetitions, switch to the right side. To increase intensity, add extra sets of pulses.

3. **QUADRICEPS EXTENSION** *(strengthens the muscles in the front of your thighs*

Lie on your back with your knees bent, feet flat on the floor, and arms resting alongside your body. Your shoulders, arms, and neck should stay relaxed.

Slowly straighten your right knee, keeping the thigh aligned with the thigh of your left leg. Do not lock the knee. Slowly return to the starting position. Alternate legs after each set.

4. **BUTT-BUSTERS** *(tones the butt and back of your thighs).*

Get down on all fours, with your right knee bent and aligned under your hip. Extend your left leg behind you, with the toe touching the floor. Bend your elbows so that your forearms and hands rest on the floor. Be sure your elbows are aligned under your shoulders and that your head, with eyes downward, is aligned with your spine

Slowly lift your left leg so the thigh is parallel to the floor, while simulta-neously tightening the buttock. Do not lift any higher, or you will place strain on your lower back. Do not arch your back, and do not lock your knee. Lower the leg almost to the floor, without touching down. After you've done three sets with one leg, repeat with the other leg.

5. **PARALLEL SQUAT** *(tones the quadriceps, hamstrings, and gluteal muscles)*
Note: You may find it easier to squat if you do so against a wall. As you continue to perform this exercise, your quadriceps will lengthen over time, allowing you to remain in this position longer. Do not perform this exercise if you feel pain in your knees.

Take a dumbbell in each hand. Stand with your feet a little closer than hip distance apart, knees slightly bent. Hold the weights at your sides. Squat down by sitting back as though you were lowering yourself into a chair. Keep your back straight. To avoid knee stress, be sure your weight is firmly in your heels.

Lower yourself until your thighs are parallel to the floor (no lower), to a count of four. Do not let your knees bend so far that they extend beyond your toes. Tighten your buttocks, and press up to the starting position, for a count of four.

get to know the glycemic index

When you are following a low-carbohydrate diet, you want to make the best choices on your limited carbohydrate budget. That typically means choosing carbohydrates that are digested slowly and, therefore, raise your blood sugar slowly. The slower your blood sugar rises, the theory goes, the less insulin will be released. Since insulin stores glucose and helps convert excess glucose to body fat, the less of it released the better.

How do you know which carbohydrates cause your blood sugar to spike and which raise it more slowly? Well, there are some general guidelines. Whole-grain foods, for instance, are digested more slowly than foods that are highly refined. Foods with lots of added sugar will probably raise your blood sugar level more quickly than foods with less sugar or small amounts of naturally occurring sugars.

But there's another, much more precise, way to determine how a particular food will affect your blood sugar levels. You can use the glycemic index, which is a ranking of foods by the amount that they raise blood sugar levels. There are two different types of rankings: One assigns a glycemic index (GI) value of 100 to white bread and then compares all other foods to it. Foods that are converted to sugar more slowly than white bread have lower GI values, while foods that are converted faster have higher values. Another method of ranking GI values is to assign glucose a GI of 100. In that case, foods are compared to the effect of glucose at raising blood sugar. No matter which method is used, the idea is the same. The GI value of a food lets you compare its effect on your blood sugar relative to other foods. That can help you make wiser food choices.

To get the values for each individual food listed in the glycemic index, researchers had a group of healthy people eat the food, and then tested their blood for glucose levels two to three hours later. The food was then assigned a GI number based on the rapidity with which it raised blood sugar levels compared to either white bread or glucose. Foods that caused a rapid and marked increase in blood sugar were assigned high glycemic index values (70 and above), while those that had slower and less dra-

High Glycemic Index Foods		Moderate Glycemic Index Foods		Low Glycemic Index Foods	
Glucose	100	Orange Juice	57	Apple	36
Baked Potato	85	White Rice	56	Pear	36
Corn Flakes	84	Popcorn	55	Skim Milk	32
Cheerios	74	Corn	55	Green Beans	30
Graham Crackers	74	Brown Rice	55	Lentils	29
Honey	73	Sweet Potato	54	Kidney Beans	27
Watermelon	72	(Ripe) Banana	50	Grapefruit	25
White Bread/Bagel	70–72	Orange	43	Barley	25
Table Sugar	65	Apple Juice	41		
Raisins	64				

Reprinted by permission of www.healthchecksystems.com.

matic effects on blood sugar levels were assigned low glycemic index values (55 and lower).

There are only a few nutrition research groups in the world that have tested the glycemic response and compiled GI values. We've included a sample chart, above, to give you some idea of the comparative glycemic value of some common foods. For further information about the glycemic index and a searchable database of foods, visit the University of Sydney's website at www.glycemicindex.com.

A caveat: The way a food is prepared can affect its GI. Pasta cooked al dente (firm) is absorbed more slowly than pasta that is cooked longer. Adding fat (butter to a potato, for instance) will decrease the GI of a food because it slows its effect on blood sugar. The same is true of adding protein or foods with organic acids, such as yogurt and pickles, to a meal. All of these slow down the conversion of carbohydrates into sugars.

pay attention to portion size

A basic premise of low-carb dieting is that we eat too much carbohydrate. But most weight-control experts believe there is a yet more important reason behind our ever-expanding waistlines: We eat too much, period. Even when we are trying to lose weight, we tend to underestimate the total amount of food we eat. Researchers have discovered, for example, that dieters who thought they weren't losing weight because they had a "slow metabolism" were actually eating double the amount of food they thought they were consuming. Just because you're eating foods with fewer carbs doesn't mean you can eat unlimited amounts of them. In order to lose weight, you must take in fewer calories than your body needs so it is forced to burn fat for fuel. So no matter which low-carb program you follow—indeed, no matter what type of weight-loss plan you use—you must pay attention to portion size.

How do you know if the bran muffin you ate or the bowl of cereal you poured this morning is a single serving or more like five servings? You have to keep tabs on how much you eat, measuring and weighing for a while until your eyes (and your stomach) get used to true portion sizes.

Start out by measuring and weighing the foods you eat most frequently. A food scale for weighing portions and a set of measuring cups and spoons will provide you with the information you need. Read food labels and use the accompanying charts to find out how much of a food is in a standard serving. (You may be surprised to discover how much smaller a standard serving of steak is compared to the portions generally served in restaurants and even at family barbecues.) This may all seem tedious at first. But once you become familiar with what a serving looks like, you'll be able to judge food on sight with minimum effort, even at parties and restaurants. Eventually, you will only have to weigh or measure foods from time to time to spot-check for accuracy.

Standard servings

Bread, Cereal, Rice, and Pasta (Grains)
1 slice bread
1 ounce ready-to-eat cereal
½ cup cooked cereal, rice, or pasta

Fruit
1 medium piece raw fruit (an apple, banana, or peach, for example)
½ cup cut-up raw fruit
½ cup canned fruit
¾ cup fruit juice

Vegetables
1 cup raw, leafy vegetables
½ cup cut-up raw vegetables
½ cup cooked vegetables
¾ cup vegetable juice

Meat, Poultry, Fish, Dry Beans, Eggs, and Nuts
2–3 ounces cooked, lean meat, poultry, or fish
½ cup cooked dry beans (equal to 1 ounce of meat)
1 egg (equal to 1 ounce of meat)
2 tablespoons peanut butter (equal to 1 ounce of meat)

Milk, Yogurt, and Cheese
1 cup milk or yogurt
1½ ounces natural cheese
2 ounces processed cheese

If you find that your helpings are not always standard serving sizes, gradually cut back. For example, if you normally have three slices of bacon, just have two instead. Also, try to serve yourself standard portion sizes by dividing larger portions into smaller servings on your plate, so you can develop an eye for what is a normal portion. For example, pour only one ounce of cereal to familiarize yourself with how much that is. And be honest with yourself—if you're not sure about a portion size, it's best to overestimate it and reduce the amount you actually eat.

Here are some other suggestions for satisfying yourself with smaller portions:

- Remove serving dishes, bowls, and platters from the table during meals. If the food is right there, it's easy to take a few more bites. Measure out your portions before bringing food to the table. If this isn't possible, move serving dishes out of your reach on the dining table.
- Use smaller plates, bowls, and glasses to make your portions look

larger. For example, put your entree on a salad plate instead of a dinner plate. Eat cereal from a cup rather than a bowl. One study showed that 70 percent of the people in a weight-reduction program were more satisfied with less food when it was served on a salad plate than when it was served on a dinner plate.

- Serve fiber-rich, high-bulk foods at the beginning of the meal. Try a hearty salad, fresh fruit, or crunchy raw vegetables for starters. This may help you feel satisfied with far fewer calories and minimize that famished feeling so you have better control during the rest of the meal.
- Take small bites and chew thoroughly. Swallow what is in your mouth before preparing the next bite.
- Leave some food uneaten at each meal—a few peas, a spoonful of rice, or a bite of meat—to break the "clean plate" habit.
- Get rid of leftovers immediately. Many dieters eat more calories after the meal is over.

An eye for portions

When dining or snacking away from home, weighing or measuring your food isn't very practical, so use these handy visuals to estimate the size of portions:

Clenched fist = 1 cup fresh fruit, uncooked vegetables, pasta, or rice

Thumb = 1 ounce cheese or cooked meat

Tip of thumb = 1 teaspoon mayonnaise, margarine, or butter

Golf ball = ¼ cup nuts or dried fruit

Deck of cards = 3 ounces cooked meat or poultry

Checkbook = 3 ounces cooked fish

Computer mouse = 1 small baked potato

Baseball = 1 cup cereal or yogurt

Tennis ball = ½ cup serving cooked cereal, rice, pasta, or ice cream

measure your success

As you progress on your diet plan, you'll want to measure your progress toward your weight-loss goal. But it's important to include more than a daily trip to the bathroom scale in that evaluation.

get real

The first step is to make sure the expectations you begin with are realistic and good for you physically and mentally. We would all love to drop all our extra pounds in a week, of course. But you have to remember that you didn't put the extra pounds on overnight, so you can't expect to lose them overnight. Losing a large amount of weight in a very short amount of time generally means that something is wrong—either with your diet plan, your health, or more likely, both. Aim to lose ½ to 2 pounds a week. Taking off more than that will not only put your health at risk, it will lower your chances of keeping that weight off in the long run.

When setting your goal you need to know what a healthy weight is for you and how far away you are from that goal. That's true even if your main motivation for losing weight is your appearance. People who are at a healthy weight tend to look good. Besides, it simply makes no sense to risk vitamin deficiencies, bone loss, fatigue, dehydration, eating disorders, and a host of other health troubles for the sake of achieving some model-thin physique. Face it, for the vast majority of us, that waiflike look simply isn't feasible or healthy, nor is it necessarily all that attractive, despite what advertisers might have us believe. Achieving a healthy weight, on the other hand, brings with it a lowered risk of high blood pressure, diabetes, heart disease, and other health problems.

figure your BMI

How do you determine what healthy weight to aim for? One of the most widely accepted methods is the Body Mass Index, or BMI. For most people, the BMI reflects the amount of body fat better than the weight on the scale does. It can also better gauge the effect your weight has on your health. (However, BMI is not a good gauge of body fat in people who have lots of muscle.)

Here's how to calculate your BMI:
1) Weigh yourself first thing in the morning, without clothes.

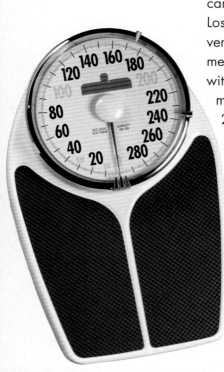

2) Confirm your height, in inches.

3) Multiply your weight in pounds by 703.

4) Divide the result in step 3 by your height in inches.

5) Divide the result in step 4 by your height in inches again. The resulting number is your BMI.

A BMI between 18.5 and 24.9 is in the healthy range; it's associated with the least risk of disease. A BMI between 25 and 29.9 indicates that you are overweight, while a BMI of 30 or more means that you're obese and have a much greater risk of certain diseases such as heart disease, high blood pressure, and type 2 diabetes.

To then find out if your goal weight—the weight that you would like to get down to—is a healthy one, work the equation again, this time substituting your goal weight for your current weight. If the resulting BMI for your goal weight falls within the healthy range, then it's a reasonable one. If it falls below or above that range, adjust your goal weight until it's within the healthy range. Once you've determined what healthy weight to shoot for, subtract it from your current weight, and you'll know how many pounds you need to lose to get there.

use more than the scale

Use your bathroom scale once a week to track your progress—but don't obsess over it. There's no sense in weighing yourself every day. The weight on the scale can fluctuate in response to water retention and other factors, so any daily changes may not indicate a loss (or gain) of body fat. And, as you build muscle through exercise, your weight may actually stay the same or increase because muscle weighs more than fat. If there are weeks when the number on the scale doesn't budge, you may have exchanged pounds of fat for pounds of muscle—a success and one that will make it easier for you to continue burning calories. Muscle is more dense than fat, so it takes up less room. Your jeans may not be as tight or your watchband may be looser. Check the mirror to see if it reflects progress.

If you don't notice a difference, double-check your efforts. Look back at the past couple of weeks in your food diary to see whether you started to eat larger portions or more empty carbs, or if you're exercising less. If that's the case, don't get down on yourself. Just rededicate yourself to your diet and exercise program.

Your body also may have hit a plateau. This can occur without an obvious reason. Increasing your exercise intensity may help, but sometimes you just have to ride it out. Stick to your eating and exercise regime, and you should start losing again. Rest assured that such weight-loss pauses are normal stops on the path to a healthy weight.

the nutrient counter

Thank you, Uncle Sam

This nutrient counter was adapted from: U.S. Department of Agriculture, Agricultural Research Service. 2011. USDA Nutrient Database for Standard Reference, Release 16. Nutrient Data Laboratory Home Page, http://www.nal.usda.gov/fnic/foodcomp

Variety is key to a healthy diet. Variety in the foods you eat helps ensure you get a full range of the vitamins, minerals, and other nutrients that are so important for health. Variety can also be the difference between a successful weight-loss plan and one that is too boring to be tolerated for long.

How do you make eating a pleasure when you're on a diet that restricts carbohydrates? At first, it may seem easy, because you get to have higher-fat foods—steaks and such—that are often discouraged in traditional weight-loss plans. But after awhile, even these foods can lose their allure. You need to expand your food horizons, going beyond processed foods and empty carbs to explore the abundance of delicious and nutritious whole foods.

That's where this nutrient counter comes in. The counter lists nutrient values for hundreds of foods with varying amounts of carbs, so you can compare foods side-by-side to decide which fit best in your weight-loss plan.

For each food item, the counter lists the calories and the number of grams of total carbohydrate, fiber, protein, total fat, and saturated fat in a portion. (While the total carbohydrate value for a food includes its fiber content, we've broken out the number of fiber grams where available so you can see how many of a food's carb grams come from beneficial, indigestible fiber.) Values have been rounded to the nearest whole number. If "Tr" (which stands for trace) appears in a column, it means there's less than half a gram of that nutrient in a single portion of that food. If "na" appears, that means the value was not available to us. When comparing foods, remember to check the portion sizes listed to be sure you're looking at equal portions of each food.

The counter can also help you deal with reality. Despite your best intentions, there may be times when your food choices are not exactly low carb. Instead of giving up on your diet because you simply couldn't pass up that fresh-baked Vienna bread or you just didn't want to say no to a slice of your surprise birthday cake, you can account for it. Use the counter to get an idea of how many extra grams of carbohydrate you took in, then look for lower-carb foods for the rest of the meal or the next few meals to help balance it out and get back on track.

FOOD, PORTION	CAL	TOTAL CARB (G)	FIBER (G)	PROTEIN (G)	TOTAL FAT (G)	SAT FAT (G)
BAKED PRODUCTS						
Bagels, plain (includes onion, poppy, sesame), 1 medium	270	53	2	11	2	Tr
Biscuits, plain or buttermilk, 1 medium	186	25	1	3	8	1
Bread, cornbread, made with low-fat (2%) milk, 1 piece	173	28	na	4	5	1
Bread, French or Vienna (includes sourdough), 1 slice, medium	175	33	2	6	2	Tr
Bread, Italian, 1 slice, medium	54	10	1	2	1	Tr
Bread, mixed-grain (includes whole-grain, 7-grain), 1 slice	65	12	2	3	1	Tr
Bread, pita, whole-wheat, 1 small	74	15	2	3	1	Tr
Bread, raisin, 1 slice	71	14	1	2	1	Tr
Bread, rye, 1 slice	83	15	2	3	1	Tr
Bread, white, 1 slice	80	15	1	2	1	Tr
Bread, whole-wheat, 1 slice	80	15	3	3	1	Tr
Brownies, 2″ square	227	36	1	3	9	2
Cake, angel food, 1/12 of 12 oz	72	16	Tr	2	Tr	Tr
Cake, chocolate, without frosting, 1/12 of 9″ dia	340	51	2	5	14	5
Cake, pound, 1/12 of 12 oz	109	14	Tr	2	6	3
Cake, white, 1/12 of 9″ dia	264	42	1	4	9	2
Cheesecake, 1/6 of 17 oz	257	20	Tr	4	18	8
Cookies, chocolate chip, 1 (3½″–4″ dia) cookie	190	26	1	2	9	4
Cookies, chocolate sandwich, with creme filling, 1 cookie	160	25	1	Tr	2	Tr
Cookies, fortune, 1 cookie	30	7	Tr	Tr	Tr	Tr

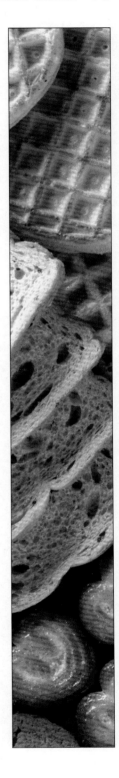

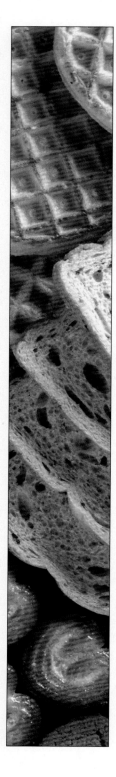

Food, portion	Cal	Total Carb (g)	Fiber (g)	Protein (g)	Total Fat (g)	Sat Fat (g)
Baked Products *(cont.)*						
Cookies, oatmeal, 1 cookie	61	10	Tr	1	2	1
Cookies, peanut butter, 1 cookie	72	9	Tr	1	4	1
Cookies, sugar, 1 cookie	66	8	Tr	1	3	1
Crackers, cheese, 1 small cracker (1" square)	5	1	Tr	Tr	Tr	Tr
Crackers, cheese, sandwich with peanut butter filling, 1 sandwich	32	4	Tr	1	2	Tr
Crackers, crispbread, rye, 1 crispbread	37	8	2	1	Tr	Tr
Crackers, matzo, plain, 1 matzo	111	23	1	3	Tr	Tr
Crackers, saltines, 1 cracker, (2" square)	13	2	Tr	Tr	Tr	Tr
Crackers, wheat, 1 thin square	9	1	Tr	Tr	Tr	Tr
Crackers, whole-wheat, 1 cracker	18	3	Tr	Tr	1	Tr
Croissants, butter, 1 croissant	231	26	1	5	12	7
Croutons, ½ cup	93	13	1	2	4	1
Danish pastry, fruit, 1 pastry	263	34	1	4	13	3
Doughnuts, cake, plain, frosted, or chocolate-coated, 1 doughnut	204	21	1	2	13	3
Doughnuts, yeast-leavened, glazed, 1 doughnut	242	27	1	4	14	3
English muffins, enriched (includes sourdough), 1 muffin	134	26	2	4	1	Tr
Fig bars, 1 cookie	56	11	1	1	1	Tr

FOOD, PORTION	CAL	TOTAL CARB (G)	FIBER (G)	PROTEIN (G)	TOTAL FAT (G)	SAT FAT (G)
BAKED PRODUCTS *(CONT.)*						
French toast, made with low-fat (2%) milk, 1 slice	149	16	na	5	7	2
Graham crackers, 1 square (2½″)	30	5	Tr	Tr	1	Tr
Ice cream cones, wafer, 1 cone	17	3	Tr	Tr	Tr	Tr
Ice cream cones, sugar, 1 cone	40	8	Tr	1	Tr	Tr
Muffins, blueberry, 1 medium	313	54	3	6	7	2
Muffins, corn, 1 medium	345	58	4	7	9	2
Pancakes, 1 pancake (4″ dia)	74	14	Tr	2	1	Tr
Pie, apple, ⅙ of 8″ dia	277	40	2	2	13	4
Pie, pecan, ⅛ of 9″ dia	503	64	na	6	27	5
Rolls, dinner, whole-wheat, 1 roll	96	18	3	3	2	Tr
Rolls, burger or hotdog, 1 bun	120	21	1	4	2	Tr
Rolls, hard, Kaiser, 1 roll, (3½″ dia)	167	30	1	6	2	Tr
Sweet rolls, cinnamon, with raisins, 1 roll, 2¾″ square	223	31	1	4	10	2
Taco shells, baked, 1 medium	62	8	1	1	3	Tr
Toaster pastries, fruit, 1 pastry	204	37	1	2	5	1
Tortillas, corn, 1 tortilla, 1 oz	62	13	2	2	1	Tr
Tortillas, flour, 1 tortilla, 7–8″ dia	150	26	2	4	3	1
Waffles, plain, frozen, ready-to-heat, 1 waffle square	98	15	1	2	3	1
BEEF PRODUCTS						
Beef, ground, 85% lean/15% fat, broiled, 1 patty (¼ lb raw)	193	0	0	20	12	5
Beef, ground, 95% lean/5% fat, broiled, 1 patty (¼ lb raw)	140	0	0	22	5	3
Bottom round, braised, 3 oz	234	0	0	24	14	5

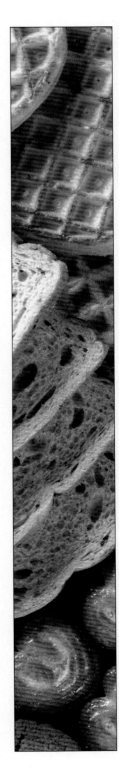

Food, portion	Cal	Total Carb (g)	Fiber (g)	Protein (g)	Total Fat (g)	Sat Fat (g)
Beef Products *(cont.)*						
Bottom sirloin butt, broiled, 3 oz	213	0	0	26	11	4
Brisket, whole, braised, 3 oz	327	0	0	20	27	11
Chuck, arm roast, braised, 3 oz	282	0	0	23	20	8
Corned beef, brisket, cured, cooked, 3 oz	213	Tr	0	15	16	5
Eye of round, roasted, 3 oz	195	0	0	23	11	4
Liver, pan-fried, 3 oz	142	4	0	21	4	1
Rib, eye, broiled, 3 oz	174	0	0	25	8	3
Rib, prime, roasted, 3 oz	361	0	0	18	31	13
Shank crosscuts, simmered, 3 oz	224	0	0	26	12	5
Short loin, porterhouse steak, broiled, 3 oz	280	0	0	19	22	9
Skirt steak, broiled, 3 oz	174	0	0	23	9	3
Tenderloin, broiled, 3 oz	247	0	0	21	17	7
Top round, broiled, 3 oz	195	0	0	26	9	3
Top sirloin, broiled, 3 oz	219	0	0	24	13	5
Beverages						
Beer, light, 12 fl oz	99	5	0	1	0	0
Beer, regular, 12 fl oz	150	13	0	2	0	0
Carbonated beverage, diet or sugar-free, with nonnutritive sweeteners, 12 fl oz	0	0	0	Tr	0	0
Chocolate syrup, 2 tbsp	109	25	1	1	Tr	Tr
Chocolate-flavor beverage mix for milk, powder, 1 serving	80	21	1	1	1	Tr
Citrus fruit juice drink, frozen concentrate, prepared with water, 8 fl oz	124	30	Tr	Tr	Tr	0
Clam and tomato juice, 5.5 oz	80	18	Tr	1	Tr	Tr

Food, portion	Cal	Total Carb (g)	Fiber (g)	Protein (g)	Total Fat (g)	Sat Fat (g)
Beverages *(cont.)*						
Club soda, 12 fl oz	0	0	0	0	0	0
Cocoa mix, no sugar added, powder, 1 envelope	56	10	1	2	Tr	Tr
Cocoa mix, powder, 3 heaping tsp	111	24	1	2	1	1
Coffee, brewed from grounds, 8 fl oz	2	0	0	Tr	0	0
Coffee, instant, regular, prepared with water, 6 fl oz	4	1	0	Tr	0	Tr
Coffee, instant, with sugar, cappuccino-flavor powder, 1 serving envelope	107	20	Tr	1	2	1
Coffee substitute, cereal grain beverage, prepared with water, 8 fl oz	12	2	1	Tr	Tr	Tr
Cola, carbonated, 12 fl oz	155	40	0	Tr	0	0
Cranberry juice cocktail, 8 fl oz	144	36	Tr	0	Tr	Tr
Cranberry-apple juice drink, 8 fl oz	174	44	Tr	Tr	Tr	0
Cream soda, 12 fl oz	189	49	0	0	0	0
Fruit punch drink, frozen concentrate, prepared, 8 fl oz	114	29	Tr	Tr	0	Tr
Ginger ale, 12 fl oz	124	32	0	0	0	0
Grape juice, 8 fl oz	150	37	na	Tr	0	0
Hard liquor (gin, rum, vodka, whiskey), distilled, 80 proof, 1 jigger (1.5 fl oz)	97	0	0	0	0	0
Lemonade, low-calorie, powder, prepared, 8 fl oz	5	1	0	Tr	0	0
Lemonade, frozen concentrate, prepared, 8 fl oz	131	34	Tr	Tr	Tr	Tr

Food, portion	Cal	Total Carb (g)	Fiber (g)	Protein (g)	Total Fat (g)	Sat Fat (g)
Beverages *(cont.)*						
Liqueur, coffee, 53 proof, 1 jigger (1.5 fl oz)	175	24	0	Tr	Tr	Tr
Pineapple and grapefruit juice drink, canned, 8 fl oz	118	29	Tr	1	Tr	Tr
Pineapple and orange juice drink, canned, 8 fl oz	125	30	Tr	3	0	0
Rice beverage, RICE DREAM, canned, 1 cup	120	25	0	Tr	2	Tr
TABASCO Tomato Cocktail, mild, ready-to-drink, 8 fl oz	56	12	1	2	0	0
Tea, brewed, 8 fl oz	2	1	0	0	0	Tr
Tea, herb, brewed, 6 fl oz	2	Tr	0	0	0	Tr
Tea, instant, unsweetened, powder, prepared, 8 fl oz	2	Tr	0	Tr	0	0
Tonic water, 12 fl oz	124	32	na	0	0	0
Water, 8 fl oz	0	0	0	0	0	0
Wine, dessert, sweet, 3.5 fl oz	165	14	0	Tr	0	0
Wine, table, 3.5 fl oz	79	3	0	Tr	0	0
Cereals, Grains, and Pasta						
Bran flakes, ¾ cup	96	24	5	3	1	Tr
CHEERIOS, 1 cup	111	22	3	3	2	Tr
Corn grits, white, cooked with water, 1 cup	143	31	1	3	Tr	Tr
CREAM OF WHEAT, regular, cooked with water, 1 cup	126	27	1	4	Tr	Tr
CRISPIX, 1 cup	109	25	Tr	2	Tr	Tr
FIBER ONE, ½ cup	59	24	14	2	1	Tr
GOLDEN GRAHAMS, ¾ cup	112	25	1	2	1	Tr
GRAPE-NUTS, ½ cup	208	47	5	6	1	Tr

Food, portion	Cal	Total Carb (g)	Fiber (g)	Protein (g)	Total Fat (g)	Sat Fat (g)
Cereals, Grains, and Pasta (cont.)						
HONEY BUNCHES OF OATS, ¾ cup	118	25	1	2	2	Tr
KELLOGG'S Corn Flakes, 1 cup	101	24	1	2	Tr	Tr
KELLOGG'S FROSTED MINI-WHEATS, bite size, 1 cup	189	45	6	6	1	Tr
KELLOGG'S Raisin Bran, 1 cup	195	47	7	5	2	Tr
Multi-Bran CHEX, 1 cup	166	41	6	3	1	Tr
NATURE VALLEY LOW FAT FRUIT GRANOLA, ⅔ cup	212	44	3	4	3	Tr
Oats, instant, plain, prepared with water, cooked, 1 cup	129	22	4	5	2	Tr
POST BANANA NUT CRUNCH, 1 cup	249	44	4	5	6	1
POST FRUIT & FIBRE Dates, Raisins & Walnuts Cereal, 1 cup	212	42	5	4	3	Tr
QUAKER Low Fat 100% Natural Granola with Raisins, ½ cup	195	41	3	4	3	1
RICE KRISPIES, 1¼ cups	119	29	Tr	2	Tr	Tr
SPECIAL K, 1 cup	117	22	1	7	Tr	Tr
Wheat CHEX, 1 cup	104	24	3	3	1	Tr
Wheat germ, toasted, 1 cup	432	56	17	33	12	2
WHEATIES, 1 cup	107	24	3	3	1	Tr
Whole Grain TOTAL, ¾ cup	97	23	2	2	1	Tr
Amaranth, 1 cup	729	129	30	28	13	3
Barley, pearled, cooked, 1 cup	193	44	6	4	1	Tr
Buckwheat groats, roasted, cooked, 1 cup	155	33	5	6	1	Tr
Bulgur, cooked, 1 cup	151	34	8	6	Tr	Tr

Food, portion	Cal	Total Carb (g)	Fiber (g)	Protein (g)	Total Fat (g)	Sat Fat (g)
Cereals, Grains, and Pasta (cont.)						
Cornmeal, self-rising, bolted, plain, enriched, yellow, 1 cup	407	86	8	10	4	1
Couscous, cooked, 1 cup	176	36	2	6	Tr	Tr
Hominy, canned, white, 1 cup	119	24	4	2	1	Tr
Macaroni, cooked, enriched, 1 cup	220	45	2	7	1	Tr
Macaroni, whole-wheat, cooked, 1 cup	174	37	4	7	1	Tr
Millet, cooked, 1 cup	207	41	2	6	2	Tr
Noodles, chow mein, 1 cup	237	26	2	4	14	2
Noodles, egg, cooked, 1 cup	213	40	2	8	2	Tr
Noodles, soba, cooked, 1 cup	113	24	na	6	Tr	Tr
Oat bran, cooked, 1 cup	88	25	6	7	2	Tr
Oats, 1 cup	607	103	17	26	11	2
Quinoa, cooked, 1 cup	636	117	10	22	10	1
Rice, brown, long-grain, cooked, 1 cup	216	45	4	5	2	Tr
Rice noodles, cooked, 1 cup	192	44	2	2	Tr	Tr
Rice, white, long-grain, cooked, 1 cup	205	45	1	4	Tr	Tr
Spaghetti, cooked, 1 cup	197	40	2	7	1	Tr
Triticale, 1 cup	645	138	na	25	4	1
Wheat flour, white, bread, enriched, 1 cup	495	99	3	16	2	Tr
Wheat flour, whole-grain, 1 cup	407	87	15	16	2	Tr
Wild rice, cooked, 1 cup	166	35	3	7	1	Tr
Dairy Products						
Cheese, blue, 1 oz	100	1	0	6	8	5

Food, portion	Cal	Total Carb (g)	Fiber (g)	Protein (g)	Total Fat (g)	Sat Fat (g)
Dairy Products *(cont.)*						
Cheese, brie, 1 oz	95	Tr	0	6	8	5
Cheese, cheddar or colby, 1 oz	114	Tr	0	7	9	6
Cheese, cottage, creamed, 1 cup (not packed)	232	6	0	28	10	6
Cheese, cottage, low-fat, 1% milkfat, 1 cup (not packed)	163	6	0	28	2	1
Cheese, cream, 1 tbsp	51	Tr	0	1	5	3
Cheese, feta, crumbled, 1 cup	396	6	0	21	32	22
Cheese food, pasteurized process, American, 1 oz	94	2	0	5	7	4
Cheese, low-fat, cheddar or colby, 1 oz	49	1	0	7	2	1
Cheese, mozzarella, part skim, 1 oz	72	1	0	7	5	3
Cheese, parmesan, grated, 1 tbsp	22	Tr	0	2	1	1
Cheese, provolone, 1 oz	98	1	0	7	7	5
Cheese, ricotta, part skim, ½ cup	171	6	0	14	10	6
Cheese, swiss, 1 oz	108	2	0	8	8	5
Cream, half-and-half, 1 tbsp	20	1	0	Tr	2	1
Cream, half-and-half, fat-free, 1 individual (.5 fl oz) container	9	1	0	Tr	Tr	Tr
Cream, light (coffee or table), 1 individual container	22	Tr	0	Tr	2	1
Cream, sour, 1 tbsp	26	1	0	Tr	3	2
Cream, whipped, topping, pressurized, 1 tbsp	8	Tr	0	Tr	1	Tr

Food, portion	Cal	Total Carb (g)	Fiber (g)	Protein (g)	Total Fat (g)	Sat Fat (g)
Dairy Products *(cont.)*						
Egg substitute, liquid, ¼ cup	29	1	0	6	0	0
Egg, whole, fried or scrambled, 1 large	92	Tr	0	6	7	2
Egg, whole, hard-boiled	78	0	0	6	5	2
Eggnog, 1 cup	343	34	0	10	19	11
Milk, 2%, 1 cup	122	11	0	8	5	2
Milk, buttermilk, low-fat, 1 cup	98	12	0	8	2	1
Milk, canned, evaporated, 1 cup	338	25	0	17	19	12
Milk, canned, evaporated, nonfat, 1 cup	200	29	0	19	1	Tr
Milk, chocolate, low-fat, 1 cup	180	26	1	8	5	3
Milk, fat-free or skim, 1 cup	83	12	0	8	Tr	Tr
Milk shakes, chocolate, 10.6 oz	357	63	1	9	8	5
Milk, whole, 3.25%, 1 cup	146	11	0	8	8	5
Yogurt, fruit, low-fat, 8 fl oz	243	46	0	10	3	2
Yogurt, plain, nonfat, 8 fl oz	137	19	0	14	Tr	Tr
Yogurt, vanilla, low-fat, 8 fl oz	208	34	0	12	3	2
Fast Foods						
Biscuit, egg, cheese, and bacon, 1 biscuit	477	33	na	16	31	11
Cheeseburger, large, double patty, with condiments and vegetables, 1 sandwich	704	40	na	38	44	18
Cheeseburger, large, single patty, with bacon and condiments, 1 sandwich	608	37	na	32	37	16
Cheeseburger, double patty, with condiments and vegetables, 1 sandwich	417	35	na	21	21	9

FOOD, PORTION	CAL	TOTAL CARB (G)	FIBER (G)	PROTEIN (G)	TOTAL FAT (G)	SAT FAT (G)
FAST FOODS *(CONT.)*						
Cheeseburger, single patty, with condiments, 1 sandwich	295	27	na	16	14	6
Chicken, breaded and fried, boneless nuggets, with bbq sauce, 6 pieces	330	25	0	17	18	6
Chicken, breaded and fried, dark meat, 2 pieces	431	16	na	30	27	7
Chicken, breaded and fried, light meat, 2 pieces	494	20	na	36	30	8
Chicken fillet sandwich, plain, 1 sandwich	515	39	na	24	29	9
Chili con carne, 8 fl oz	256	22	na	25	8	3
Chimichanga, beef and cheese, 1 chimichanga	443	39	na	20	23	11
Coleslaw, ¾ cup	147	13	na	1	11	2
Crab cake, 1 cake	160	5	Tr	11	10	2
Croissant, egg and cheese, 1 croissant	368	24	na	13	25	14
Enchilada, cheese and beef, 1 enchilada	323	30	na	12	18	9
Fish fillet, battered or breaded, fried, 1 fillet	211	15	Tr	13	11	3
Fish sandwich, with tartar sauce, 1 sandwich	431	41	na	17	23	5
French toast sticks, 5 pieces	513	58	3	8	29	5
Frijoles with cheese, 1 cup	225	29	na	11	8	4
Hamburger, double patty, with condiments, 1 sandwich	576	39	na	32	32	12
Hamburger, single patty, with condiments, 1 sandwich	272	34	2	12	10	4
Hotdog, plain, on bun	242	18	na	10	15	5

Food, portion	Cal	Total Carb (g)	Fiber (g)	Protein (g)	Total Fat (g)	Sat Fat (g)
Fast Foods *(cont.)*						
Hotdog, with chili, on bun	296	31	na	14	13	5
Hotdog, with corn flour coating (corndog)	460	56	na	17	19	5
Hush puppies, 5 pieces	257	35	na	5	12	3
Ice milk, vanilla, soft-serve, with cone, 1 cone	164	24	Tr	4	6	4
Nachos, with cheese, 1 portion (6–8 nachos)	346	36	na	9	19	8
Nachos, with cheese, beans, ground beef, and peppers, 1 portion (6–8 nachos)	569	56	na	20	31	12
Onion rings, breaded and fried, 1 portion (8–9 onion rings)	276	31	na	4	16	7
Pizza with cheese, 1 slice	140	21	na	8	3	2
Pizza with cheese, meat, and vegetables, 1 slice	184	21	na	13	5	2
Potato, baked, with cheese sauce and bacon, 1 serving	451	44	na	18	26	10
Potato, baked, with cheese sauce and broccoli, 1 serving	403	47	na	14	21	9
Potato, baked, with sour cream and chives, 1 serving	393	50	na	7	22	10
Potato, french fried in vegetable oil, 1 small order	291	34	3	4	16	3
Potato salad, ⅓ cup	108	13	na	1	6	1
Roast beef sandwich, plain, 1 sandwich	346	33	na	22	14	4
Roast beef sandwich with cheese, 1 sandwich	473	45	na	32	18	9
Salad, vegetable, tossed, without dressing, ¾ cup	17	3	na	1	Tr	Tr

Food, portion	Cal	Total Carb (g)	Fiber (g)	Protein (g)	Total Fat (g)	Sat Fat (g)
Fast Foods *(cont.)*						
Salad, vegetable, tossed, without dressing, with cheese and egg, 1½ cups	102	5	na	9	6	3
Salad, vegetables, tossed, without dressing, with turkey, ham and cheese, 1½ cups	267	5	na	26	16	8
Shrimp, breaded and fried, 1 portion (6–8 shrimp)	454	40	na	19	25	5
Submarine sandwich, with cold cuts, 1 submarine	456	51	na	22	19	7
Submarine sandwich, with roast beef, 1 submarine	410	44	na	29	13	7
Submarine sandwich, with tuna salad, 1 submarine	584	55	na	30	28	5
Taco, 1 small	369	27	na	21	21	11
Taco salad, 1½ cups	279	24	na	13	15	7
Fats and Oils						
Butter, salted, 1 tbsp	102	Tr	0	Tr	12	6
Lard, 1 tbsp	115	0	0	0	13	5
Margarine, stick or tub, 80% fat, 1 tbsp	100	Tr	0	Tr	11	2
Margarine spread, fat-free, tub, 1 tbsp	6	1	0	Tr	Tr	Tr
Margarine, vegetable oil spread, stick/tub/bottle, 60% fat, 1 tbsp	75	0	0	Tr	8	1
Oil (olive, peanut, sesame, soybean), 1 tbsp	120	0	0	0	14	2
Oil, vegetable (canola, corn, safflower, sunflower), 1 tbsp	120	0	0	0	15	Tr
Salad dressing, French, 1 tbsp	73	2	0	Tr	7	1

Food, portion	Cal	Total Carb (g)	Fiber (g)	Protein (g)	Total Fat (g)	Sat Fat (g)
Fats and Oils *(cont.)*						
Salad dressing, French, reduced-fat, 1 tbsp	37	5	Tr	Tr	2	Tr
Salad dressing, Italian, 1 tbsp	43	2	0	Tr	4	1
Salad dressing, thousand island, 1 tbsp	59	2	Tr	Tr	6	1
Salad dressing, vinegar and oil, 1 tbsp	72	Tr	0	0	8	1
Finfish and Shellfish Products						
Anchovy, European, canned in oil, drained, 1 anchovy	8	0	0	1	Tr	Tr
Bass, striped, cooked, 3 oz	105	0	0	19	3	1
Catfish, cooked, 3 oz	89	0	0	16	2	1
Clam, raw, 1 medium	11	Tr	0	2	Tr	Tr
Cod, Atlantic, cooked, 3 oz	70	0	0	15	1	Tr
Crab, Alaska king, cooked, 1 leg	130	0	0	26	2	Tr
Crab, Alaska king, imitation, made from surimi, 3 oz	87	9	0	10	1	Tr
Crab, dungeness, cooked, moist heat, 1 crab	140	1	0	28	2	Tr
Crayfish, wild, cooked, moist heat, 3 oz	70	0	0	14	1	Tr
Dolphinfish, cooked, 3 oz	93	0	0	20	1	Tr
Fish sticks, frozen, preheated, 1 stick (4"×1"×½")	76	7	Tr	4	3	1
Flatfish (flounder and sole), cooked, 1 fillet	149	0	0	31	2	Tr
Gefiltefish, sweet recipe, 1 piece	35	3	0	4	1	Tr
Halibut, cooked, 3 oz	119	0	0	23	2	Tr
Herring, Atlantic, cooked, 3 oz	173	0	0	20	10	2

Food, portion	Cal	Total Carb (g)	Fiber (g)	Protein (g)	Total Fat (g)	Sat Fat (g)
Finfish and Shellfish Products (cont.)						
Orange roughy, 3 oz, cooked	59	0	0	12	1	Tr
Oyster, Eastern, breaded/ fried, 6 medium	173	10	0	8	11	3
Perch or Pike, cooked, 3 oz	99	0	0	21	1	Tr
Salmon, smoked (lox), 1 oz	33	0	0	5	1	Tr
Salmon, pink, canned, solids with bone and liquid, 3 oz	118	0	0	17	5	1
Salmon, sockeye, cooked, 3 oz	184	0	0	23	9	2
Sardine, Atlantic, canned in oil, drained, with bone, 1 small	25	0	0	3	1	Tr
Scallops, breaded/fried, 2 large	67	3	0	6	3	1
Shrimp, 1 medium	6	Tr	0	1	Tr	Tr
Snapper, cooked, 3 oz	109	0	0	22	1	Tr
Surimi, 3 oz	84	6	0	13	1	Tr
Trout, rainbow, wild, cooked, 3 oz	128	0	0	19	5	1
Tuna, fresh, bluefin, cooked, 3 oz	156	0	0	25	5	1
Tuna, light, canned in water, drained, 1 can	191	0	0	42	1	Tr
Tuna, white, canned in water, drained, 1 can	220	0	0	41	5	1
Whitefish, smoked, 3 oz	92	0	0	20	1	Tr
Fruits and Fruit Juices						
Apple juice, unsweetened, 1 cup	117	29	Tr	Tr	Tr	Tr
Apples, raw, with skin, 1 medium (3 per lb.)	72	19	3	Tr	Tr	Tr
Applesauce, sweetened, 1 cup	194	51	3	Tr	Tr	Tr

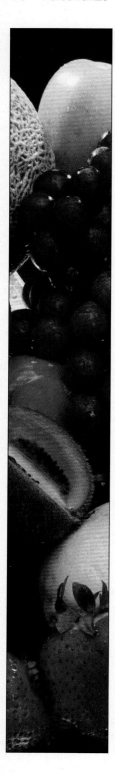

Food, portion	Cal	Total Carb (g)	Fiber (g)	Protein (g)	Total Fat (g)	Sat Fat (g)
Fruits and Fruit Juices *(cont.)*						
Apricots, juice pack, with skin, halves, 1 cup	117	30	4	2	Tr	Tr
Apricots, dried, stewed, without added sugar, halves, 1 cup	213	55	7	3	Tr	Tr
Apricots, raw, 1 apricot	17	4	1	Tr	Tr	Tr
Avocados, raw, 1 cup, puréed	368	20	15	5	34	5
Bananas, raw, 1 medium	105	27	3	1	Tr	Tr
Blackberries, raw, 1 cup	62	14	8	2	1	Tr
Blueberries, raw, 1 cup	83	21	3	1	Tr	Tr
Cantaloupe, raw, ⅛ melon	23	6	1	1	Tr	Tr
Cherries, sweet, raw, 1 cherry	4	1	Tr	Tr	Tr	Tr
Cranberry sauce, canned, sweetened, 1 slice (½" thick)	86	22	1	Tr	Tr	Tr
Dates, deglet noor, 1 date	23	6	1	Tr	Tr	Tr
Dates, medjool, pitted, 1 date	66	18	2	Tr	Tr	0
Figs, raw, 1 medium (2¼" dia)	37	10	1	Tr	Tr	Tr
Fruit cocktail, juice pack, 1 cup	109	28	2	1	Tr	Tr
Grape juice, sweetened, 1 cup	128	32	Tr	Tr	Tr	Tr
Grapefruit juice, white, canned, sweetened, 1 cup	115	28	Tr	1	Tr	Tr
Grapefruit, raw, ½ medium	41	10	1	1	Tr	Tr
Grapes, red or green, raw, seedless, 1 grape	3	1	Tr	Tr	Tr	Tr
Honeydew, ⅛ of 5¼" dia melon	45	11	1	1	Tr	Tr
Kiwi fruit, skinless, 1 medium	46	11	2	1	Tr	Tr
Lemon juice, 1 lemon's yield	12	4	Tr	Tr	0	0
Mangos, raw, 1 fruit	135	35	4	1	1	Tr

FOOD, PORTION	CAL	TOTAL CARB (G)	FIBER (G)	PROTEIN (G)	TOTAL FAT (G)	SAT FAT (G)
FRUITS AND FRUIT JUICES *(CONT.)*						
Nectarines, raw, 1 (2½″ dia)	60	14	2	1	Tr	Tr
Olives, ripe, canned, 1 large	5	Tr	Tr	Tr	Tr	Tr
Orange juice, canned, unsweetened, 1 cup	105	25	Tr	1	Tr	Tr
Oranges, raw, 1 medium	62	15	3	1	Tr	Tr
Peach nectar, canned, 1 cup	134	35	1	1	Tr	Tr
Peaches, canned, juice pack, halves or slices, 1 cup	109	29	3	2	Tr	Tr
Peaches, raw, 1 (2½″ dia)	58	14	2	1	Tr	Tr
Pears, canned, juice pack, 1 half, with liquid	38	10	1	Tr	Tr	Tr
Pears, raw, 1 medium pear	96	26	5	1	Tr	Tr
Pineapple, canned, juice pack, 1 cup, crushed, sliced, or chunks	149	39	2	1	Tr	Tr
Pineapple juice, canned, unsweetened, 1 cup	140	34	1	1	Tr	Tr
Pineapple, raw, 1 slice	40	11	1	Tr	Tr	Tr
Plantains, raw, 1 medium	218	57	4	2	1	Tr
Plums, raw, 1 fruit (2⅛″ dia)	30	8	1	Tr	Tr	Tr
Prune juice, canned, 1 cup	182	45	3	2	Tr	Tr
Quinces, raw, 1 fruit	52	14	2	Tr	Tr	Tr
Raisins, seedless, 1 oz (60 raisins)	85	22	2	Tr	Tr	Tr
Raspberries, raw, 10 berries	10	2	1	Tr	Tr	Tr
Rhubarb, raw, diced, 1 cup	26	6	2	1	Tr	Tr
Strawberries, whole, 1 cup	46	11	Tr	Tr	Tr	Tr
Tangerines, raw, 1 medium	37	9	2	1	Tr	Tr
Watermelon, raw, ¹⁄₁₆ of melon	86	22	1	2	Tr	Tr

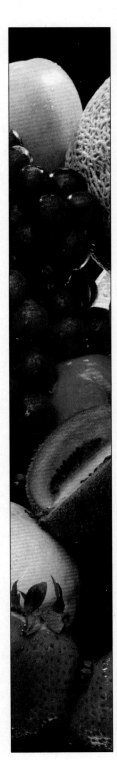

Food, portion	Cal	Total Carb (g)	Fiber (g)	Protein (g)	Total Fat (g)	Sat Fat (g)
Lamb and Veal						
Lamb, ground, broiled, 3 oz	241	0	0	21	17	7
Lamb, leg (shank and sirloin), roasted, 3 oz	219	0	0	22	14	6
Lamb, shoulder (arm and blade), roasted, 3 oz	235	0	0	19	17	7
Veal, boneless breast, braised, 3 oz	226	0	0	23	14	6
Veal, ground, broiled, 3 oz	146	0	0	21	6	3
Veal, shoulder, roasted, 3 oz	156	0	0	22	7	3
Legumes and Legume Products						
Bacon, meatless, 1 strip	16	Tr	Tr	1	1	Tr
Beans, baked, canned, plain or vegetarian, 1 cup	236	52	13	12	1	Tr
Beans, baked, canned, with pork and sweet sauce, 1 cup	281	53	13	13	4	1
Beans, black, boiled, 1 cup	227	41	15	15	1	Tr
Beans, great Northern, boiled, 1 cup	209	37	12	15	1	Tr
Beans, kidney, boiled, 1 cup	225	40	11	15	1	Tr
Beans, navy, boiled, 1 cup	258	48	12	16	1	Tr
Chickpeas (garbanzo beans), boiled, 1 cup	269	45	12	15	4	Tr
Chili with beans, canned, 1 cup	287	30	11	15	14	6
Cowpeas (blackeyes, crowder, Southern), boiled, 1 cup	198	35	11	13	1	Tr
Falafel, home-prepared, 1 patty	57	5	na	2	3	Tr
HARVEST BURGER, Original Flavor, All Vegetable Protein Patties, 1 patty	138	7	6	18	4	1

FOOD, PORTION	CAL	TOTAL CARB (G)	FIBER (G)	PROTEIN (G)	TOTAL FAT (G)	SAT FAT (G)
LEGUMES AND LEGUME PRODUCTS *(CONT.)*						
Hummus, 1 tbsp	27	3	1	1	1	Tr
Lentils, boiled, 1 cup	230	40	16	18	1	Tr
Lima beans, large, boiled, 1 cup	216	39	13	15	1	Tr
Miso, 1 cup	567	77	15	32	17	2
Noodles, Chinese, cellophane, or long rice (mung beans), dehydrated, 1 cup	491	121	1	Tr	Tr	Tr
Peanut butter, chunky or smooth, 2 tbsp	190	7	2	8	16	3
Peanuts, dry-roasted, without salt, 1 cup	854	31	12	35	73	10
Peas, split, boiled, 1 cup	231	41	16	16	1	Tr
Refried beans, canned, 1 cup	237	39	13	14	3	1
Sausage, meatless, 1 link	64	2	1	5	5	1
Soy milk, fluid, 1 cup	120	11	3	9	5	1
Soy sauce (tamari), 1 tbsp	11	1	Tr	2	Tr	Tr
Soybeans, mature, raw, 1 cup	774	56	17	68	37	5
Tempeh, 1 cup	320	16	na	31	18	4
Tofu, firm, prepared with calcium sulfate and magnesium chloride (nigari), ¼ block	62	2	Tr	7	4	1
Tofu, salted and fermented (fuyu), 1 block	13	1	na	1	1	Tr
NUT AND SEED PRODUCTS						
Almonds, 1 cup, whole	827	28	17	30	72	6
Brazilnuts, dried, unblanched, 1 cup shelled (32 kernels)	918	17	11	20	93	21
Cashew nuts, dry-roasted, with salt added, 1 cup	786	45	4	21	63	13

Food, portion	Cal	Total Carb (g)	Fiber (g)	Protein (g)	Total Fat (g)	Sat Fat (g)
Nut and Seed Products (cont.)						
Coconut meat, dried, sweetened, flaked, packaged, 1 cup	351	35	3	2	24	21
Hazelnuts or filberts, 10 nuts	88	2	1	2	9	1
Macadamia nuts, dry-roasted, 1 oz (10–12 kernels)	203	4	2	2	22	3
Mixed nuts, oil-roasted, with peanuts, salt added, 1 cup	876	30	13	24	80	12
Pecans, 1 oz (20 halves)	196	4	3	3	20	2
Pine nuts, dried, 10 nuts	11	Tr	Tr	Tr	1	Tr
Pistachio nuts, dry-roasted, without salt added, 1 cup	702	34	13	26	57	7
Pumpkin and squash seed kernels, dried, 1 cup	747	25	5	34	63	12
Sesame butter, tahini, 1 tbsp	89	3	1	3	8	1
Sunflower seed kernels, dried, without hulls, 1 cup	821	27	15	33	71	7
Walnuts, English, 7 nuts	183	4	2	4	18	2
Pork Products						
Backribs, fresh, roasted, 1 piece	810	0	0	53	65	24
Bacon, cured, pan-fried, 1 slice	42	Tr	0	3	3	1
Canadian-style bacon, cured, grilled, 2 slices (6 per 6-oz pkg)	87	1	0	11	4	1
Ground pork, cooked, 3 oz	252	0	0	22	18	7
Ham, cured, boneless, extra-lean (approx 5% fat), roasted, 3 oz	123	1	0	18	5	2
Ham, cured, regular (approx 13% fat), canned, roasted, 3 oz	192	Tr	0	17	13	4
Ham shank, fresh, roasted, 3 oz	246	0	0	22	17	6
Loin, blade (chops), fresh, bone-in, pan-fried, 1 chop	284	0	0	18	23	8

Food, portion	Cal	Total Carb (g)	Fiber (g)	Protein (g)	Total Fat (g)	Sat Fat (g)
Pork Products *(cont.)*						
Loin, country-style ribs, fresh, braised, 1 piece	696	0	0	56	51	19
Loin, fresh, sirloin (roasts), boneless, roasted, 3 oz	176	0	0	24	8	3
Spareribs, braised, 1 piece	703	0	0	51	54	20
Poultry Products						
Chicken, breast, meat and skin, batter-fried, ½ breast	364	13	Tr	35	18	5
Chicken, breast, meat and skin, roasted, ½ breast	193	0	0	29	8	2
Chicken, canned, no broth, 5 oz can	230	1	0	32	10	3
Chicken, drumstick, meat and skin, batter-fried, 1 drumstick	193	6	Tr	16	11	3
Chicken, drumstick, meat and skin, roasted, 1 drumstick	112	0	0	14	6	2
Chicken, leg, meat and skin, batter-fried, 1 leg	431	14	Tr	34	26	7
Chicken, leg, meat and skin, roasted, 1 leg	264	0	0	30	15	4
Chicken, roasting, light meat only, roasted, 1 cup chopped	214	0	0	38	6	2
Chicken, wing, meat and skin, batter-fried, 1 wing	159	5	Tr	10	11	3
Chicken, wing, meat and skin, roasted, 1 wing	99	0	0	9	7	2
Cornish game hens, meat and skin, roasted, 1 whole bird	668	0	0	57	47	13
Duck, roasted, ½ duck	1287	0	0	73	108	37
Turkey, breast, meat and skin, roasted, ½ breast	1633	0	0	248	64	18

Food, portion	Cal	Total Carb (g)	Fiber (g)	Protein (g)	Total Fat (g)	Sat Fat (g)
Poultry Products (cont.)						
Turkey, ground, cooked, 1 patty (4 oz raw)	193	0	0	22	11	3
Turkey, leg, meat and skin, roasted, 1 leg	1136	0	0	152	54	17
Sausages and Luncheon Meats						
Beef, cured, sausage, cooked, smoked, 1 sausage	134	1	0	6	12	5
Beef, thin sliced, 5 slices	37	1	0	6	1	Tr
Bologna, beef, 1 oz slice	87	1	0	3	8	3
Bologna, turkey, 1 slice	59	1	Tr	3	4	1
Bratwurst, pork, cooked, 1 link	281	2	0	12	25	9
Frankfurter, beef, 1 frankfurter	149	2	0	5	13	5
Ham, sliced, extra-lean (approx 5% fat), 1 slice	37	Tr	0	5	1	Tr
LOUIS RICH, Turkey Bacon, 1 oz serving	35	Tr	0	2	3	1
Pastrami, cured, 1 slice (1 oz)	98	1	0	5	8	3
Pepperoni, pork/beef, 15 slices	135	1	Tr	6	12	5
Salami, cooked, beef, 1 slice	67	Tr	0	3	6	3
Salami, dry or hard, pork, 1 slice (3⅛" dia × ⅟₁₆" thick)	41	Tr	0	2	3	1
Sausage, Italian, pork, cooked, 1 link (4 links per lb)	268	1	0	17	21	8
Sausage, smoked link, pork and beef, 1 piece (4" long × 1⅛" dia)	218	2	0	8	20	7
Turkey breast meat, 1 oz slice	28	0	0	6	Tr	Tr
Snacks						
Banana chips, 1 oz	147	17	2	1	10	8
Beef jerky, 1 piece, large	82	2	Tr	7	5	2

Food, portion	Cal	Total Carb (g)	Fiber (g)	Protein (g)	Total Fat (g)	Sat Fat (g)
Snacks (*cont.*)						
BETTY CROCKER Fruit Roll Ups, berry flavored, 2 rolls	104	24	na	Tr	1	Tr
CHEX mix, 1 oz (approx ⅔ cup)	120	18	2	3	5	2
Corn chips, plain, 1 bag (7 oz)	1067	113	10	13	66	9
Granola bar, hard, peanut, 1 oz	136	18	1	3	6	1
Granola bar, soft, uncoated, nut and raisin, 1 bar (1 oz)	127	18	2	2	6	3
Popcorn, air-popped, 1 cup	31	6	1	1	Tr	Tr
Popcorn, caramel-coated, with peanuts, 1 oz (approx ⅔ cup)	113	23	1	2	2	Tr
Potato chips, plain, salted, 8 oz	1217	120	10	16	79	25
Pretzels, hard, salted, 10 twists	229	48	2	5	2	Tr
Tortilla chips, plain, 1 oz	142	18	2	2	7	1
Soups, Sauces, and Gravies						
Gravy, beef or brown, 1 serving	25	4	Tr	1	1	Tr
Gravy, turkey, canned, 1 tbsp	8	1	Tr	Tr	Tr	Tr
Sauce, barbecue, 8 fl oz	188	32	3	5	5	1
Sauce, cheese, ¼ cup	110	4	Tr	4	8	4
Sauce, hoisin, 1 tbsp	35	7	Tr	1	1	Tr
Sauce, pasta, spaghetti/ marinara, 1 cup	143	21	4	4	5	1
Sauce, salsa, ½ cup	36	8	2	2	Tr	Tr
Sauce, teriyaki, 1 tbsp	15	3	Tr	1	0	0
Sauce, Worcestershire, 1 tbsp	11	3	0	0	0	0
Soup, bean with ham, canned, chunky, ready-to-serve, 8 fl oz	231	27	11	13	9	3
Soup, beef broth or bouillon, canned, ready-to-serve, 1 cup	17	Tr	0	3	1	Tr

Food, portion	Cal	Total Carb (g)	Fiber (g)	Protein (g)	Total Fat (g)	Sat Fat (g)
Soups, Sauces, and Gravies *(cont.)*						
Soup, beef noodle, canned, prepared with equal volume water, 8 fl oz	83	9	1	5	3	1
Soup, black bean, canned, prepared with equal volume water, 1 cup	116	20	4	6	2	Tr
Soup, chicken noodle, canned, prepared with equal volume water, 8 fl oz	75	9	1	4	2	1
Soup, chicken vegetable, chunky, ready-to-serve, 8 fl oz	166	19	na	12	5	1
Soup, chicken with rice, canned, prepared with equal volume water, 8 fl oz	60	7	1	4	2	Tr
Soup, clam chowder, New England, canned, prepared with equal volume milk, 1 cup	164	17	1	9	7	3
Soup, cream of mushroom, canned, prepared with equal volume milk, 8 fl oz	203	15	Tr	6	14	5
Soup, minestrone, canned, prepared with equal volume water, 8 fl oz	82	11	1	4	3	1
Soup, split pea with ham, chunky, ready-to-serve, 1 cup	185	27	4	11	4	2
Soup, tomato, canned, prepared with equal volume water, 8 fl oz	85	17	Tr	2	2	Tr
Soup, vegetable beef, canned, prepared with equal volume water, 8 fl oz	78	10	Tr	6	2	1
Sweets						
AFTER EIGHT Mints, 1 piece	29	6	Tr	Tr	1	1

Food, portion	Cal	Total Carb (g)	Fiber (g)	Protein (g)	Total Fat (g)	Sat Fat (g)
Sweets (cont.)						
BABY RUTH Bar, 1 bar (0.75 oz)	97	13	1	1	5	3
Caramels, 1 piece	39	8	Tr	Tr	1	1
Frosting, chocolate, creamy, ready-to-eat, 2 tbsp	163	26	Tr	Tr	7	2
Frozen juice novelties, fruit and juice bars, 1 bar (2.5 fl oz)	63	16	1	1	Tr	0
Frozen yogurt, chocolate or vanilla, soft-serve, ½ cup (4 fl oz)	116	18	2	3	4	3
Gelatin dessert, dry mix, prepared with water, ½ cup	84	19	0	2	0	0
Gelatin dessert, sugar-free, prepared with water, ½ cup	10	0	0	1	0	0
Gumdrops, 10 gummy bears	87	22	Tr	0	0	0
Honey, 1 tbsp	64	17	Tr	Tr	0	0
Ice cream, low-fat, chocolate, vanilla, or strawberry, ½ cup	143	19	1	3	5	2
Ice novelties, Italian ice, ½ cup	61	16	0	Tr	Tr	0
Jams, jellies, and preserves, 1 tbsp	56	14	Tr	Tr	Tr	Tr
M&M's Milk Chocolate Candies, 10 pieces	34	5	Tr	Tr	1	1
M&M's Peanut Chocolate Candies, 10 pieces	103	12	1	2	5	2
Marshmallows, 1 regular	23	6	Tr	Tr	Tr	Tr
Milk chocolate, 1 bar (1.55 oz)	235	26	1	3	13	6
MILKY WAY Bar, 1 bar (.8 oz)	97	16	Tr	1	4	2
NESTLÉ CRUNCH, 1.4 oz	209	26	1	2	11	6
Peanut bar, 1 bar (1.4 oz)	209	19	2	6	13	2
Puddings, chocolate, ready-to-eat, 1 can (5 oz)	197	33	1	4	6	1

Food, portion	Cal	Total Carb (g)	Fiber (g)	Protein (g)	Total Fat (g)	Sat Fat (g)
Sweets *(cont.)*						
Puddings, JELL-O Brand Fat-Free Sugar-Free Instant Reduced-Calorie Pudding & Pie Filling, chocolate, powder, 1 serving	34	8	1	1	Tr	Tr
Puddings, rice, ready-to-eat, 1 can (5 oz)	231	31	Tr	3	11	2
Puddings, tapioca, ready-to-eat, 1 snack size (4 oz)	134	22	Tr	2	4	1
Puddings, vanilla, ready-to-eat, 1 snack size (4 oz)	146	25	0	3	4	1
REESE'S Peanut Butter Cups, 2 cups (1.6 oz package)	232	25	2	5	14	5
Semisweet chocolate chips, 1 cup (6 oz package)	805	106	10	7	50	30
Sherbet, orange, ½ cup (4 fl oz)	107	22	2	1	1	1
Sugars, brown, 1 cup, packed	829	214	0	0	0	0
Sugars, granulated, 1 tsp	16	4	0	0	0	0
Sugars, granulated, 1 cup	774	200	0	0	0	0
Sugars, powdered, 1 tbsp	31	8	0	0	Tr	Tr
Syrups, chocolate, fudge, 2 tbsp	133	24	1	2	3	2
Syrups, pancake, 1 tbsp	47	12	Tr	0	0	0
YORK Peppermint Pattie, 1 patty (1.5 oz)	165	35	1	1	3	2
Vegetables and Vegetable Products						
Artichoke hearts, boiled, ½ cup	42	9	5	3	Tr	Tr
Asparagus, boiled, 4 spears	13	2	1	1	Tr	Tr
Bamboo shoots, boiled, 1 cup	14	2	1	2	Tr	Tr
Beans, lima, canned, ½ cup	88	17	4	5	Tr	Tr

Food, portion	Cal	Total Carb (g)	Fiber (g)	Protein (g)	Total Fat (g)	Sat Fat (g)
Vegetables and Vegetable Products *(cont.)*						
Beans, snap, green, boiled, 1 cup	44	10	4	2	Tr	Tr
Beets, boiled, slices, ½ cup	37	8	2	1	Tr	Tr
Broccoli, raw, 1 cup chopped	30	6	2	2	Tr	Tr
Brussels sprouts, boiled, 1 sprout	8	1	1	1	Tr	Tr
Cabbage, Chinese (pak choi), boiled, shredded, 1 cup	20	3	2	3	Tr	Tr
Cabbage, raw, shredded, 1 cup	17	4	2	1	Tr	Tr
Carrots, baby, raw, 1 small	4	1	Tr	Tr	Tr	Tr
Carrots, raw, 1 medium	25	6	2	1	Tr	Tr
Catsup, 1 tbsp	14	4	Tr	Tr	Tr	Tr
Cauliflower, boiled, ½ cup	14	3	2	1	Tr	Tr
Cauliflower, raw, 1 floweret	3	1	Tr	Tr	Tr	Tr
Celery, raw, 1 medium stalk	6	1	1	Tr	Tr	Tr
Coleslaw, ½ cup	41	7	1	1	2	Tr
Collards, boiled, chopped, 1 cup	49	9	5	4	1	Tr
Corn pudding, 1 cup	273	32	na	11	13	6
Corn, sweet, boiled, 1 ear	83	19	2	3	1	Tr
Corn, sweet, canned, whole kernel, 1 cup	133	30	3	4	2	Tr
Cucumber, ½ cup slices	8	2	Tr	Tr	Tr	Tr
Eggplant, boiled, 1 cup cubes	35	9	2	1	Total	Tr
Kale, cooked, chopped, 1 cup	36	7	3	2	1	Tr
Lettuce, butterhead or iceberg, 1 leaf	1	Tr	Tr	Tr	Tr	Tr
Lettuce, cos or romaine, 1 leaf	2	Tr	Tr	Tr	Tr	Tr
Mung beans, sprouted, stir-fried, 1 cup	62	13	2	5	Tr	Tr

Food, portion	Cal	Total Carb (g)	Fiber (g)	Protein (g)	Total Fat (g)	Sat Fat (g)
Vegetables and Vegetable Products *(cont.)*						
Mushrooms, boiled, ½ cup pieces	22	4	2	2	Tr	Tr
Mushrooms, raw, 1 medium	4	1	Tr	1	Tr	Tr
Okra, boiled, ½ cup slices	18	4	2	1	Tr	Tr
Onion rings, breaded, pan-fried, frozen, heated in oven, 10 rings	244	23	1	3	16	5
Onions, boiled, 1 cup	92	21	3	3	Tr	Tr
Peas and carrots, boiled, ½ cup	38	8	2	2	Tr	Tr
Peas, green, boiled, 1 cup	134	25	9	9	Tr	Tr
Peppers, jalapeno, 1 pepper	4	1	Tr	Tr	Tr	Tr
Peppers, sweet, green, raw, 1 medium	24	6	2	1	Tr	Tr
Pickle, dill, 1 medium	12	3	1	Tr	Tr	Tr
Pickle, sweet, 1 midget gherkin	7	2	Tr	Tr	Tr	Tr
Pickle relish, hotdog, 1 tbsp	14	4	Tr	Tr	Tr	Tr
Potato pancakes, 1 pancake	207	22	2	5	12	2
Potato salad, 1 cup	358	28	3	7	21	4
Potatoes, au gratin, 1 cup	323	28	4	12	19	12
Potatoes, baked, flesh, 1 potato	145	34	2	3	Tr	Tr
Potatoes, french fried, frozen, oven-heated, 10 strips	100	16	2	2	4	1
Potatoes, hashed brown, 1 cup	413	55	5	5	20	2
Potatoes, mashed, whole milk added, 1 cup	174	37	3	4	1	1
Pumpkin, canned, 1 cup	83	20	7	3	1	Tr
Rutabagas, cooked, boiled, 1 cup cubes	66	15	3	2	Tr	Tr
Sauerkraut, canned, 1 cup	27	6	4	1	Tr	Tr

Food, portion	Cal	Total Carb (g)	Fiber (g)	Protein (g)	Total Fat (g)	Sat Fat (g)
Vegetables and Vegetable Products *(cont.)*						
Spinach, frozen, chopped or leaf, boiled, ½ cup	30	5	4	4	Tr	Tr
Squash, summer, all varieties, raw, sliced, 1 cup	18	4	1	1	Tr	Tr
Squash, winter, acorn, baked, cubes, 1 cup	115	30	9	2	Tr	Tr
Squash, winter, butternut, baked, cubes, 1 cup	82	22	na	2	Tr	Tr
Succotash, boiled, 1 cup	221	47	9	10	2	Tr
Sweet potato, baked in skin, 1 medium	103	24	4	2	Tr	Tr
Sweet potato, candied, 1 piece	144	29	3	1	3	1
Tomato juice, canned, with salt added, 1 cup	41	10	1	2	Tr	Tr
Tomato paste, canned, 1 cup	215	50	12	11	1	Tr
Tomato sauce, with mushrooms, canned, 1 cup	86	21	4	4	Tr	Tr
Tomato sauce, with onions, green peppers, and celery, canned, 1 cup	103	22	4	2	2	Tr
Tomatoes, stewed, 1 cup	66	16	3	2	Tr	Tr
Tomatoes, raw, 1 cup, chopped	32	7	2	2	Tr	Tr
Tomatoes, sun-dried, packed in oil, drained, 1 cup	234	26	6	6	15	2
Vegetable juice cocktail, 1 cup	46	11	2	2	Tr	Tr
Vegetables, mixed, frozen, boiled, ½ cup	59	12	4	3	Tr	Tr
Waterchestnuts, Chinese (matai), raw, slices, ½ cup slices	60	15	2	1	Tr	Tr
Yam, baked, cubes, 1 cup	158	38	5	2	Tr	Tr

enjoy low-carb recipes

You'll love eating low carb with the scrumptious recipes in this section. They're light on carbs but packed with flavor. And with the nutritional information provided with each one, you'll know how each dish fits in your low-carb plan. The preparation times are based on the approximate amount of time that is needed to assemble the recipe before cooking, baking, chilling, or serving. They include prep steps, such as measuring, mixing, and chopping. (If some preparation and cooking can be done simultaneously, that's taken into account.) Preparation of optional ingredients and serving suggestions is not included.

great-start breakfasts

ham & cheddar frittata

3 eggs
3 egg whites
½ teaspoon salt
½ teaspoon freshly ground black pepper
1½ cups (4 ounces) frozen broccoli florets, thawed
6 ounces deli smoked ham, cut into ½-inch cubes (1¼ cups)
⅓ cup drained bottled roasted red bell peppers, cut into thin strips
1 tablespoon butter
½ cup (2 ounces) shredded sharp Cheddar cheese

1. Preheat broiler.

2. Beat eggs, egg whites, salt and pepper in large bowl until blended. Stir in broccoli, ham and pepper strips.

3. Melt butter over medium heat in 10-inch ovenproof skillet with sloping side. Pour egg mixture into skillet; cover. Cook 5 to 6 minutes or until eggs are set around edge. (Center will be wet.)

4. Uncover; sprinkle cheese over frittata. Transfer skillet to broiler; broil, 5 inches from heat source, 2 minutes or until eggs are set in center and cheese is melted. Let stand 5 minutes; cut into wedges. *Makes 4 servings*

baked eggs

4 eggs
4 teaspoons milk
Salt and black pepper to taste

1. Preheat oven to 375°F. Grease 4 small baking dishes or custard cups.

2. Break 1 egg into each dish. Add 1 teaspoon milk to each dish. Sprinkle with salt and pepper.

3. Bake about 15 minutes or until set. *Makes 4 servings*

Baked Egg Options: Top eggs with desired amount of one or more of the following before baking; half-and-half, salsa, shredded cheese, chopped ham, minced chives or minced fresh herbs. Bake as directed above.

ham & cheddar frittata

brunch eggs olé

8 eggs
½ cup all-purpose flour
1 teaspoon baking powder
¾ teaspoon salt
2 cups (8 ounces) shredded Monterey Jack cheese with jalapeño peppers
1½ cups (12 ounces) small curd cottage cheese
1 cup (4 ounces) shredded sharp Cheddar cheese
1 jalapeño pepper,* seeded and chopped
½ teaspoon hot pepper sauce
Fresh Salsa (recipe follows)

*Jalapeño peppers can sting and irritate the skin; wear rubber gloves when handling peppers and do not touch eyes. Wash hands after handling.

1. Preheat oven to 350°F. Grease 9-inch square baking pan.

2. Beat eggs in large bowl at high speed with electric mixer 4 to 5 minutes or until slightly thickened and lemon colored.

3. Combine flour, baking powder and salt in small bowl. Stir flour mixture into eggs until blended.

4. Combine Monterey Jack cheese, cottage cheese, Cheddar cheese, jalapeño and hot pepper sauce in medium bowl; mix well. Fold into egg mixture until well blended. Pour into prepared pan.

5. Bake 45 to 50 minutes or until golden brown and firm in center. Let stand 10 minutes before cutting into squares to serve. Serve with Fresh Salsa. Garnish as desired.

Makes 8 servings

fresh salsa

3 medium plum tomatoes, seeded and chopped
2 tablespoons chopped onion
1 small jalapeño pepper,* stemmed, seeded and minced
1 tablespoon chopped fresh cilantro
1 tablespoon lime juice
¼ teaspoon salt
⅛ teaspoon black pepper

*Jalapeño peppers can sting and irritate the skin; wear rubber gloves when handling peppers and do not touch eyes. Wash hands after handling.

Stir together tomatoes, onion, jalapeño pepper, cilantro, lime juice, salt and black pepper in small bowl. Refrigerate until ready to serve.

Makes 1 cup

brunch eggs olé

nutrients per
serving:

Calories: 334
Carbohydrate: 11 g
Calories From Fat: 65%
Total Fat: 24 g
Cholesterol: 469 mg
Sodium: 362 mg
Dietary Fiber: 1 g
Protein: 19 g

apple and brie omelet

2 large Golden Delicious apples
2 tablespoons butter or margarine, divided
½ teaspoon ground nutmeg
4 ounces Brie cheese
8 large eggs, lightly beaten
2 green onions, thinly sliced

1. Place large serving platter in oven and preheat to 200°F. Peel, core and slice apples; place in microwavable container. Top with 1 tablespoon butter and nutmeg. Cover and microwave at HIGH (100% power) 3 minutes. Set aside. While apples cook, trim rind from cheese; thinly slice cheese.

2. Melt 1½ teaspoons butter in medium nonstick skillet over medium heat; rotate skillet to coat bottom. Place eggs in medium bowl and whisk until blended. Pour half of eggs into skillet. Let cook, without stirring, 1 to 2 minutes, or until set on bottom. With rubber spatula, lift side of omelet and slightly tilt pan to allow uncooked portion of egg flow underneath. Cover pan and cook 2 to 3 minutes, until eggs are set but still moist on top. Remove platter from oven and slide omelet into center. Spread apples evenly over entire omelet, reserving a few slices for garnish, if desired. Evenly space cheese slices over apples. Sprinkle with onion, reserving some for garnish. Return platter to oven.

3. Cook remaining beaten eggs in remaining 1½ teaspoons butter as directed above. When cooked, slide spatula around edge to be certain omelet is loose. Carefully place second omelet over cheese, apple and onion mixture. Top with reserved apple and onion slices. Cut into wedges to serve.

Makes 4 servings

apple and brie omelet

nutrients per serving:

½ of omelet

Calories: 111
Carbohydrate: 7 g
Calories From Fat: 26%
Total Fat: 3 g
Saturated Fat: <1 g
Cholesterol: 0 mg
Sodium: 538 mg
Dietary Fiber: 1 g
Protein: 13 g

greek isles omelet

Nonstick cooking spray
¼ cup chopped onion
¼ cup canned artichoke hearts, rinsed and drained
¼ cup washed and torn spinach leaves
¼ cup chopped plum tomato
1 cup cholesterol-free egg substitute
2 tablespoons sliced pitted ripe olives, rinsed and drained
Dash black pepper

1. Spray small nonstick skillet with cooking spray; heat over medium heat until hot. Cook and stir onion 2 minutes or until crisp-tender.

2. Add artichoke hearts. Cook and stir until heated through. Add spinach and tomato; toss briefly. Remove from heat. Transfer vegetables to small bowl. Wipe out skillet and spray with cooking spray.

3. Combine egg substitute, olives and pepper in medium bowl. Heat skillet over medium heat until hot. Pour egg mixture into skillet. Cook over medium heat 5 to 7 minutes; as eggs begin to set, gently lift edges of omelet with spatula and tilt skillet so that uncooked portion flows underneath.

4. When egg mixture is set, spoon vegetable mixture over half of omelet. Loosen omelet with spatula and fold in half. Slide omelet onto serving plate.

Makes 2 servings

greek isles omelet

baked eggs florentine

2 packages (10 ounces each) frozen creamed spinach
4 slices (⅛ inch thick) deli ham, about 5 to 6 ounces
4 eggs
   Salt and black pepper
⅛ teaspoon ground nutmeg
½ cup (2 ounces) shredded provolone cheese
2 tablespoons chopped roasted red pepper

1. Preheat oven to 450°F. Make small cut in each package of spinach. Microwave at HIGH 5 to 6 minutes, turning packages halfway through cooking time.

2. Meanwhile, grease 8-inch square baking pan. Place ham slices on bottom of prepared pan, overlapping slightly. Spread spinach mixture over ham slices.

3. Make 4 indentations in spinach. Carefully break 1 egg in each. Season to taste with salt and black pepper. Sprinkle with nutmeg.

4. Bake 16 to 19 minutes or until eggs are set. Remove from oven. Sprinkle cheese and red pepper over top. Return to oven and bake 1 to 2 minutes longer or until cheese is melted. Serve immediately. *Makes 4 servings*

Serving Suggestion: Serve with fresh pineapple pieces.

Prep & Cook Time: 28 minutes

baked egg florentine

chile cheese puff

¾ **cup all-purpose flour**
1½ **teaspoons baking powder**
9 **eggs**
4 **cups (16 ounces) shredded Monterey Jack cheese**
2 **cups (16 ounces) low-fat (1%) cottage cheese**
2 **cans (4 ounces each) diced green chilies, drained**
1½ **teaspoons sugar**
¼ **teaspoon salt**
⅛ **teaspoon hot pepper sauce**
1 **cup salsa**

1. Preheat oven to 350°F. Spray 13×9-inch baking dish with nonstick cooking spray.

2. Combine flour and baking powder in small bowl.

3. Whisk eggs in large bowl until blended; stir in Monterey Jack, cottage cheese, chilies, sugar, salt and hot pepper sauce. Add flour mixture; stir just until combined. Pour into prepared dish.

4. Bake, uncovered, 45 minutes or until egg mixture is set. Let stand 5 minutes before serving. Serve with salsa. *Makes 8 servings*

three-egg omelet

1 **tablespoon butter or margarine**
3 **eggs, lightly beaten**
Salt and black pepper
¼ **cup (1 ounce) shredded Cheddar cheese**
¼ **cup chopped cooked ham**

1. Melt butter in 10-inch skillet over medium heat. Add eggs; lift cooked edge with spatula to allow uncooked eggs to flow under cooked portion. Season with salt and black pepper to taste. Shake pan to loosen omelet. Cook until set.

2. Place cheese and ham on ½ of omelet. Fold omelet in half. Transfer to serving plate. Serve immediately. *Makes 1 serving*

chile cheese puff

easy brunch frittata

nutrients per serving:

Calories: 102
Carbohydrate: 11 g
Calories From Fat: 20%
Total Fat: 2 g
Saturated Fat: 1 g
Cholesterol: 7 mg
Sodium: 627 mg
Dietary Fiber: 1 g
Protein: 9 g

       Nonstick cooking spray
   1 cup small broccoli florets
2½ cups (12 ounces) frozen hash brown potatoes with onions and
       peppers (O'Brien style), thawed
1½ cups cholesterol-free egg substitute, thawed
   2 tablespoons reduced-fat (2%) milk
   ¾ teaspoon salt
   ¼ teaspoon black pepper
   ½ cup (2 ounces) shredded reduced-fat Cheddar cheese

1. Preheat oven to 450°F. Coat medium nonstick ovenproof skillet with nonstick cooking spray. Heat skillet over medium heat until hot. Add broccoli; cook and stir 2 minutes. Add potatoes; cook and stir 5 minutes.

2. Beat together egg substitute, milk, salt and pepper in small bowl; pour over potato mixture. Cook 5 minutes or until edge is set (center will still be wet).

3. Transfer skillet to oven; bake 6 minutes or until center is set. Sprinkle with cheese; let stand 2 to 3 minutes or until cheese is melted.

4. Cut into wedges; serve with sour cream, if desired. *Makes 6 servings*

deep south ham and redeye gravy

nutrients per serving:

Calories: 215
Carbohydrate: 1 g
Calories From Fat: 38%
Total Fat: 9 g
Saturated Fat: 1 g
Cholesterol: 76 mg
Sodium: 27 mg
Dietary Fiber: 1 g
Protein: 30 g

1 tablespoon butter
1 ham steak (about 1⅓ pounds)
1 cup strong coffee
¾ teaspoon sugar
¼ teaspoon hot pepper sauce

1. Heat large skillet over medium-high heat until hot. Add butter; tilt skillet to coat bottom. Add ham steak; cook 3 minutes. Turn; cook 2 minutes longer or until lightly browned. Remove ham to serving platter; set aside and keep warm.

2. Add coffee, sugar and pepper sauce to same skillet. Bring to a boil over high heat; boil 2 to 3 minutes or until liquid is reduced to ¼ cup liquid, scraping up any brown bits. Serve gravy over ham. *Makes 4 servings*

Serving Suggestion: Serve ham steak with sautéed greens and poached eggs.

easy brunch frittata

satisfying main dishes

nutrients per serving:

Calories: 205
Carbohydrate: 5 g
Calories From Fat: 39%
Total Fat: 9 g
Saturated Fat: 3 g
Cholesterol: 72 mg
Sodium: 402 mg
Dietary Fiber: <1 g
Protein: 25 g

seared beef tenderloin with horseradish-rosemary cream

1 teaspoon chili powder
½ teaspoon salt, divided
¼ teaspoon plus ⅛ teaspoon black pepper, divided
1 pound beef tenderloin
1 clove garlic, halved
  Nonstick cooking spray
⅓ cup fat-free sour cream
1 tablespoons fat-free (skim) milk
1 teaspoons reduced-fat mayonnaise
1 teaspoon prepared horseradish
½ teaspoon dried rosemary

1. Preheat oven to 425°F. Combine chili powder, ¼ teaspoon salt and ¼ teaspoon pepper in small bowl.

2. Rub tenderloin with garlic; sprinkle evenly with seasoning mixture.

3. Heat medium ovenproof skillet over medium-high heat; spray with cooking spray. Cook tenderloin 2 minutes on each side.

4. Transfer skillet to oven. Bake 30 minutes or until internal temperature of tenderloin reaches 140°F. Cover and let stand 15 minutes.

5. Meanwhile, combine sour cream, milk, mayonnaise, horseradish, rosemary, remaining ¼ teaspoon salt and ⅛ teaspoon pepper in small bowl; mix well. Cut tenderloin into 4 pieces. Top with sauce.

Makes 4 servings

seared beef tenderloin with horseradish-rosemary cream

chunky chicken and vegetable soup

nutrients per serving:

Calories: 130
Carbohydrate: 5 g
Calories From Fat: 57%
Total Fat: 8 g
Saturated Fat: 3 g
Cholesterol: 27 mg
Sodium: 895 mg
Dietary Fiber: 1 g
Protein: 9 g

  1 tablespoon vegetable oil
  1 boneless skinless chicken breast (4 ounces), diced
  ½ cup chopped green bell pepper
  ½ cup thinly sliced celery
  2 green onions, sliced
  2 cans (14½ ounces each) chicken broth
  1 cup water
  ½ cup sliced carrots
  2 tablespoons cream
  1 tablespoon finely chopped parsley
  ¼ teaspoon dried thyme leaves
  ⅛ teaspoon black pepper

1. Heat oil in large saucepan over medium heat. Add chicken; cook and stir 4 to 5 minutes or until no longer pink. Add bell pepper, celery and onions. Cook and stir 7 minutes or until vegetables are tender.

2. Add broth, water, carrots, cream, parsley, thyme and black pepper. Simmer 10 minutes or until carrots are tender. *Makes 4 servings*

peppercorn steaks

nutrients per serving:

Calories: 413
Carbohydrate: <1 g
Calories From Fat: 50%
Total Fat: 23 g
Saturated Fat: 7 g
Cholesterol: 129 mg
Sodium: 249 mg
Dietary Fiber: <1g
Protein: 49 g

  2 tablespoons olive oil
  1 to 2 teaspoons cracked red or black peppercorns or freshly
     ground pepper
  1 teaspoon minced garlic
  1 teaspoon dried herbs, such as rosemary or parsley
  4 boneless beef top loin (strip) or ribeye steaks (6 ounces each)
  ¼ teaspoon salt

1. Combine oil, peppercorns, garlic and herbs in small bowl. Rub mixture on both sides of each steak. Cover and refrigerate.

2. Prepare grill for direct cooking.

3. Place steaks on grid over medium heat. Grill, uncovered, 10 to 12 minutes for medium-rare to medium or to desired doneness, turning occasionally. Season with salt after cooking. *Makes 4 servings*

chunky chicken and vegetable soup

nutrients per serving:

Calories: 249
Carbohydrate: 10 g
Calories From Fat: 33%
Total Fat: 9 g
Saturated Fat: 1 g
Cholesterol: 147 mg
Sodium: 960 mg
Dietary Fiber: 7 g
Protein: 31 g

szechwan seafood stir-fry

1 package (10 ounces) fresh spinach leaves
4 teaspoons dark sesame oil, divided
4 cloves garlic, minced and divided
¼ cup reduced-sodium soy sauce
1 tablespoon cornstarch
1 tablespoon dry sherry or sake
1 medium red bell pepper, cut in thin 1-inch-long strips
1½ teaspoons minced fresh or bottled gingerroot
¾ pound peeled, deveined large shrimp, thawed if frozen
½ pound fresh bay scallops
2 teaspoons sesame seeds, toasted

1. Rinse spinach in cold water; drain. Heat 2 teaspoons oil in large saucepan over medium heat. Add 2 cloves garlic; stir-fry 1 minute. Add spinach; cover and steam 4 to 5 minutes or until spinach is wilted, turning with tongs after 3 minutes. Remove from heat; keep covered.

2. Meanwhile, combine soy sauce, cornstarch and sherry; stir until smooth. Set aside. Heat remaining 2 teaspoons oil in large nonstick skillet over medium-high heat. Add bell pepper; stir-fry 2 minutes. Add remaining 2 cloves garlic and ginger; stir-fry 1 minute. Add shrimp; stir-fry 2 minutes. Add scallops; stir-fry 1 minute or until shrimp and scallops are opaque. Add soy sauce mixture; stir-fry 1 minute or until sauce thickens.

3. Stir spinach mixture and transfer to 4 individual plates; top with seafood mixture and sesame seeds. *Makes 4 servings*

Tip: Substitute one large head bok choy, thinly sliced, for spinach. Increase steaming time to 8 minutes or until bok choy is tender. You may also substitute the larger and less expensive sea scallops for the bay scallops; simply cut them in quarters.

szechwan seafood stir-fry

jalapeño-lime chicken

8 chicken thighs
3 tablespoons jalapeño jelly
1 tablespoon olive oil
1 tablespoon lime juice
1 clove garlic, minced
1 teaspoon chili powder
½ teaspoon black pepper
⅛ teaspoon salt
Lime wedges (optional)

1. Preheat oven to 400°F. Line 15×10-inch jelly-roll pan with foil; spray with nonstick cooking spray.

2. Arrange chicken in single layer in prepared pan. Bake 15 minutes; drain off juices. Combine jelly, oil, lime juice, garlic, chili powder, pepper and salt in small bowl. Turn chicken; brush with half of jelly mixture. Bake 20 minutes. Turn chicken; brush with remaining jelly mixture. Bake 10 to 15 minutes or until juices run clear (180°F).

3. Garnish chicken with lime wedges, if desired.   *Makes 8 servings*

jalapeño-lime chicken

steaks with zesty merlot sauce

½ cup merlot wine
2 tablespoons Worcestershire sauce
1 tablespoon balsamic vinegar
1 teaspoon sugar
1 teaspoon beef bouillon granules
½ teaspoon dried thyme leaves
2 beef ribeye steaks (8 ounces each)
2 tablespoons finely chopped parsley

1. Combine wine, Worcestershire sauce, vinegar, sugar, bouillon granules and thyme; set aside.

2. Heat large nonstick skillet over high heat until hot. Add steaks; cook 3 minutes on each side. Turn steaks again and cook 3 to 6 minutes longer over medium heat or until desired doneness.

3. Cut steaks in half; arrange on serving platter. Place in oven to keep warm.

4. Add wine mixture to same skillet. Bring to a boil; cook and stir 1 minute, scraping up any brown bits. Spoon over steaks. Sprinkle with parsley; serve immediately.

Makes 4 servings

maple-mustard pork chops

2 tablespoons maple syrup, divided
1 tablespoon olive oil
2 teaspoons whole-grain mustard
2 center-cut pork loin chops (6 ounces each)
Nonstick cooking spray
⅓ cup water

Preheat oven to 375°F. Combine maple syrup, olive oil and mustard in small bowl. Brush syrup mixture over both sides of pork chops. Spray medium ovenproof skillet with cooking spray; heat over medium-high heat. Add chops; brown on both sides. Add water, cover and bake 20 to 30 minutes or until barely pink in center.

Makes 2 servings

steaks with zesty merlot sauce

nutrients per serving:

Calories: 200
Carbohydrate: 13 g
Calories From Fat: 32%
Total Fat: 7 g
Saturated Fat: 1 g
Cholesterol: 78 mg
Sodium: 900 mg
Dietary Fiber: 2 g
Protein: 23 g

thai noodle soup

1 package (3 ounces) ramen noodles
¾ pound chicken tenders
2 cans (about 14 ounces each) chicken broth
¼ cup shredded carrot
¼ cup frozen snow peas
2 tablespoons thinly sliced green onion tops
½ teaspoon minced garlic
¼ teaspoon ground ginger
3 tablespoons chopped fresh cilantro
½ lime, cut into 4 wedges

1. Break noodles into pieces. Cook noodles according to package directions, discarding flavor packet. Drain and set aside.

2. Cut chicken tenders into ½-inch pieces. Combine chicken broth and chicken tenders in large saucepan or Dutch oven; bring to a boil over medium heat. Cook 2 minutes.

3. Add carrot, snow peas, green onion tops, garlic and ginger. Reduce heat to low; simmer 3 minutes. Add cooked noodles and cilantro; heat through. Serve soup with lime wedges. *Makes 4 servings*

thai noodle soup

nutrients per serving:

Calories: 221
Carbohydrate: 5 g
Calories From Fat: 37%
Total Fat: 9 g
Saturated Fat: <1 g
Cholesterol: 51 mg
Sodium: 559 mg
Dietary Fiber: 2 g
Protein: 30 g

grilled red snapper
with avocado-papaya salsa

1 teaspoon ground coriander
1 teaspoon paprika
¾ teaspoon salt
⅛ to ¼ teaspoon ground red pepper
1 tablespoon olive oil
4 skinless red snapper or halibut fish fillets (5 to 7 ounces each)
½ cup diced ripe avocado
½ cup diced ripe papaya
2 tablespoons chopped cilantro
1 tablespoon fresh lime juice
4 lime wedges

1. Prepare grill for direct grilling. Combine coriander, paprika, salt and red pepper in small bowl or cup; mix well.

2. Brush oil over fish. Sprinkle 2½ teaspoons spice mixture over fish fillets; set aside remaining spice mixture. Place fish, skin side down, on oiled grid over medium-hot heat. Grill 5 minutes per side or until fish is opaque.

3. Meanwhile, combine avocado, papaya, cilantro, lime juice and reserved spice mixture in medium bowl; mix well. Serve fish with salsa and garnish with lime wedges.

Makes 4 servings

grilled red snapper with avocado-papaya salsa

nutrients per serving:

Calories: 135
Carbohydrate: 2 g
Calories From Fat: 28%
Total Fat: 4 g
Saturated Fat: 2 g
Cholesterol: 50 mg
Sodium: 144 mg
Dietary Fiber: 1 g
Protein: 22 g

roast turkey breast with spinach-blue cheese stuffing

1 frozen whole boneless turkey breast, thawed (3½ to 4 pounds)
1 package (10 ounces) frozen chopped spinach, thawed and squeezed dry
2 ounces blue cheese or feta cheese
2 ounces reduced-fat cream cheese
½ cup finely chopped green onions
4½ teaspoons Dijon mustard
4½ teaspoons dried basil leaves
2 teaspoons dried oregano leaves
Black pepper to taste
Paprika

1. Preheat oven to 350°F. Coat roasting pan and rack with nonstick cooking spray.

2. Unroll turkey breast; rinse and pat dry. Place between 2 sheets of plastic wrap. Pound turkey breast with flat side of meat mallet to about 1 inch thick. Remove and discard skin from one half of turkey breast; turn meat over so skin side (on other half) faces down.

3. Combine spinach, blue cheese, cream cheese, green onions, mustard, basil and oregano in medium bowl; mix well. Spread evenly over turkey breast. Roll up turkey so skin is on top.

4. Carefully place turkey breast on rack; sprinkle with pepper and paprika. Roast 1½ hours or until no longer pink in center of breast. Remove from oven and let stand 10 minutes before removing skin and slicing. Cut into ¼-inch slices.

Makes 14 servings (3 ounces each)

roast turkey breast with spinach-blue cheese stuffing

nutrients per serving:

Calories: 116
Carbohydrate: 15 g
Calories From Fat: 39%
Total Fat: 5 g
Saturated Fat: 1 g
Cholesterol: 4 mg
Sodium: 396 mg
Dietary Fiber: 5 g
Protein: 5 g

spaghetti squash primavera

1 teaspoon olive oil
¼ cup diced green bell pepper
¼ cup diced zucchini
¼ cup sliced mushrooms
¼ cup diced carrot
¼ cup sliced green onions
2 cloves garlic, minced
1 plum tomato, diced
1 tablespoon red wine or water
½ teaspoon dried basil leaves
¼ teaspoon salt
⅛ teaspoon black pepper
2 cups cooked spaghetti squash
2 tablespoons grated Parmesan cheese

1. Heat oil in medium skillet over low heat. Add bell pepper, zucchini, mushrooms, carrot, green onions and garlic; cook 10 to 12 minutes or until crisp-tender, stirring occasionally.

2. Stir in tomato, wine, basil, salt and black pepper; cook 4 to 5 minutes, stirring once or twice.

3. Serve vegetables over spaghetti squash. Top with cheese.   *Makes 2 servings*

spaghetti squash primavera

flank steak with italian salsa

nutrients per serving:

Calories: 191
Carbohydrate: 4 g
Calories From Fat: 54%
Total Fat: 11 g
Saturated Fat: 3 g
Cholesterol: 35 mg
Sodium: 407 mg
Dietary Fiber: 1 g
Protein: 18 g

2 tablespoons olive oil
2 teaspoons balsamic vinegar
1 lean flank steak (1½ pounds)
1 tablespoon minced garlic
¾ teaspoon salt, divided
¾ teaspoon black pepper, divided
1 cup diced plum tomatoes
⅓ cup chopped pitted kalamata olives
2 tablespoons chopped fresh basil

1. Whisk oil and vinegar in medium glass bowl until blended. Place steak in shallow dish; spread with garlic. Sprinkle ½ teaspoon salt and ½ teaspoon pepper over steak. Spoon 2 tablespoons vinegar mixture over top of steak. Marinate in refrigerator at least 20 minutes or up to 2 hours.

2. Prepare grill for direct grilling or preheat broiler. Add tomatoes, olives, basil, remaining ¼ teaspoon salt and ¼ teaspoon pepper to remaining 2 teaspoons vinegar mixture in glass bowl; mix well.

3. Drain steak; discard marinade. (Let garlic remain on steak.) Grill steak over medium-hot coals 5 to 6 minutes per side for medium-rare or until desired doneness.

4. Transfer steak to carving board. Tent with foil; let stand 5 minutes. Cut steak diagonally across grain into thin slices. Serve with tomato mixture.

Makes 6 servings

flank steak with italian salsa

nutrients per serving:

Calories: 158
Carbohydrate: 7 g
Calories From Fat: 15%
Total Fat: 3 g
Saturated Fat: <1 g
Cholesterol: 68 mg
Sodium: 304 mg
Dietary Fiber: 2 g
Protein: 26 g

main dish chicken soup

1 can (49½ ounces) fat-free, reduced-sodium chicken broth *or* 3 cans (14½ ounces each) fat-free, reduced-sodium chicken broth plus 6 ounces water
1 cup grated carrots
½ cup sliced green onions
½ cup diced red bell pepper
½ cup frozen green peas
1 seedless cucumber
½ teaspoon ground white pepper
12 chicken tenders (about 1 pound)

1. Place chicken broth (and water, if using) in large 4-quart Dutch oven. Bring to a boil over high heat. Add carrots, green onions, red pepper and green peas. Bring to a boil. Reduce heat and simmer 3 minutes.

2. Meanwhile, cut ends off cucumber and discard. Using vegetable peeler, start at top and make long, noodle-like strips of cucumber. Slice any remaining cucumber pieces thinly with knife. Add cucumber strips to Dutch oven; simmer until cucumber is tender.

3. Add chicken tenders; simmer about 5 minutes or until chicken is no longer pink.

Makes 6 servings

main dish chicken soup

nutrients per serving:

Calories: 216
Carbohydrate: 5 g
Calories From Fat: 40%
Total Fat: 9 g
Saturated Fat: 4 g
Cholesterol: 83 mg
Sodium: 420 mg
Dietary Fiber: 1 g
Protein: 27 g

pork chops paprikash

2 teaspoons butter
1 medium onion, very thinly sliced
1¼ teaspoons paprika, divided
1 teaspoon garlic salt
½ teaspoon black pepper
4 (5- to 6-ounce) bone-in center cut pork chops (about ½ inch thick)
⅓ cup well-drained sauerkraut
⅓ cup light or regular sour cream

1. Preheat broiler.

2. Melt butter in large skillet over medium heat. Separate onion slices into rings; add to skillet. Cook, stirring occasionally, until golden brown and tender, about 10 minutes.

3. Meanwhile, sprinkle 1 teaspoon paprika, garlic salt and pepper over both sides of pork chops. Place chops on rack of broiler pan.

4. Broil 4 to 5 inches from heat 5 minutes. Turn; broil 4 to 5 minutes or until chops are barely pink in center.

5. Combine cooked onion with sauerkraut, sour cream and remaining ¼ teaspoon paprika; mix well. Garnish chops with onion mixture, or spread onion mixture over chops and return to broiler. Broil just until hot, about 1 minute.   *Makes 4 servings*

pork chop paprikash

nutrients per serving:

Calories: 378

Carbohydrate: 4 g

Calories From Fat: 76%

Total Fat: 32 g

Saturated Fat: 15 g

Cholesterol: 487 mg

Sodium: 797 mg

Dietary Fiber: 1 g

Protein: 19 g

fabulous feta frittata

2 tablespoons butter or olive oil
8 eggs
¼ cup whipping cream or half-and-half
¼ cup chopped fresh basil
½ teaspoon salt
¼ teaspoon freshly ground black pepper
1 package (4 ounces) crumbled feta cheese with basil, olives and sun-dried tomatoes *or* 1 cup crumbled feta cheese
¼ cup pine nuts

1. Preheat broiler. Melt butter in 10-inch ovenproof skillet over medium heat. Tilt skillet so bottom and side are well coated with butter.

2. Beat eggs. Add cream, basil, salt and pepper; mix well. Pour mixture into skillet. Cover; cook 8 to 10 minutes or until eggs are set around edge (center will be wet).

3. Sprinkle cheese and pine nuts evenly over frittata. Transfer to broiler; broil 4 to 5 inches from heat source for 2 minutes or until center of frittata is set and pine nuts are golden brown. Cut into wedges. *Makes 4 servings*

Tip: If skillet is not ovenproof, wrap the handle in heavy-duty foil.

fabulous feta frittata

nutrients per serving:

Calories: 410
Carbohydrate: 16 g
Calories From Fat: 44%
Total Fat: 20 g
Saturated Fat: 8 g
Cholesterol: 130 mg
Sodium: 790 mg
Dietary Fiber: 1 g
Protein: 41 g

easy chicken salad

¼ **cup finely chopped celery**
¼ **cup mayonnaise**
2 **tablespoons sweet relish**
1 **tablespoon finely minced onion**
½ **teaspoon Dijon mustard**
⅛ **teaspoon salt**
   Black pepper to taste
2 **cups cubed cooked chicken**
   Salad greens (optional)

1. Combine all ingredients except chicken and salad greens in large bowl; mix well. Stir in chicken. Cover; refrigerate at least 1 hour.

2. Serve on salad greens.

Makes 2 servings

nutrients per serving:

Calories: 169
Carbohydrate: 2 g
Calories From Fat: 36%
Total Fat: 7 g
Saturated Fat: <1 g
Cholesterol: 36 mg
Sodium: 476 mg
Dietary Fiber: 4 g
Protein: 25 g

pan seared halibut steaks with avocado salsa

4 **tablespoons chipotle salsa, divided**
½ **teaspoon salt, divided**
4 **small (4 to 5 ounces)** *or* 2 **large (8 to 10 ounces) halibut steaks, cut ¾ inch thick**
½ **cup diced tomato**
½ **ripe avocado, diced**
2 **tablespoons chopped cilantro (optional)**
   Lime wedges (optional)

1. Combine 2 tablespoons salsa and ¼ teaspoon salt; spread over both sides of halibut.

2. Heat large nonstick skillet over medium heat until hot. Add halibut; cook 4 to 5 minutes per side or until fish is opaque in center.

3. Meanwhile, combine remaining 2 tablespoons salsa, ¼ teaspoon salt, tomato, avocado and cilantro, if desired, in small bowl. Mix well and spoon over cooked fish. Garnish with lime wedges, if desired.

Makes 4 servings

easy chicken salad

pasta meatball soup

10 ounces 95% ground beef sirloin
5 tablespoons acini di pepe pasta, divided
¼ cup fresh fine bread crumbs
1 egg
2 tablespoons finely chopped parsley, divided
1 teaspoon dried basil leaves, divided
¼ teaspoon salt
⅛ teaspoon black pepper
1 clove garlic, minced
2 cans (about 14 ounces each) fat-free reduced-sodium beef broth
1 (8-ounce) can tomato sauce
⅓ cup chopped onion

1. Combine beef, 2 tablespoons pasta, bread crumbs, egg, 1 tablespoon parsley, ½ teaspoon basil, salt, pepper and garlic in medium bowl. Form into approximately 28 to 30 (1-inch) meatballs.

2. Bring beef broth, tomato sauce, onion and remaining ½ teaspoon basil to a boil in large saucepan over medium-high heat. Carefully add meatballs to broth. Reduce heat to medium-low; simmer, covered, 20 minutes. Add remaining 3 tablespoons pasta; cook 10 minutes or until tender. Garnish with remaining 1 tablespoon parsley.

Makes 4 (1½-cup) servings

Tip: Acini di pepe is tiny rice-shaped pasta. You may substitute orzo pasta or pastina.

pasta meatball soup

roasted rosemary chicken legs

nutrients per serving:

Calories: 263
Carbohydrate: 2 g
Calories From Fat: 58%
Total Fat: 17 g
Saturated Fat: 5 g
Cholesterol: 77 mg
Sodium: 407 mg
Dietary Fiber: <1 g
Protein: 22 g

¼ **cup finely chopped onion**
2 **tablespoons margarine or butter, melted**
1 **tablespoon chopped fresh rosemary *or* 1 teaspoon dried rosemary**
½ **teaspoon salt**
¼ **teaspoon black pepper**
2 **cloves garlic, minced**
4 **chicken legs (about 1½ pounds)**
¼ **cup white wine or chicken broth**

1. Preheat oven to 375°F.

2. Combine onion, margarine, rosemary, salt, pepper and garlic in small bowl; set aside. Run finger under chicken skin to loosen. Rub onion mixture under and over skin. Place chicken, skin side up, in small shallow roasting pan. Pour wine over chicken.

3. Roast chicken 50 to 60 minutes or until chicken is browned and juices run clear, basting often with pan juices. Garnish as desired.   *Makes 4 servings*

curried chicken & zucchini salad

nutrients per serving:

Calories: 370
Carbohydrate: 12 g
Calories From Fat: 52%
Total Fat: 21 g
Saturated Fat: 4 g
Cholesterol: 86 mg
Sodium: 300 mg
Dietary Fiber: 1 g
Protein: 30 g

½ **cup nonfat plain yogurt**
⅓ **cup mayonnaise**
2 **tablespoons chili sauce**
1 **teaspoon white wine vinegar**
1 **teaspoon grated onion**
¾ **teaspoon curry powder**
¼ **teaspoon salt**
2 **cups shredded cooked chicken**
1 **cup seedless red grapes**
1 **medium zucchini, cut into matchstick-size strips**
   Leaf lettuce
¼ **cup slivered almonds, toasted**

1. Combine yogurt, mayonnaise, chili sauce, vinegar, onion, curry powder and salt in large bowl; stir until smooth. Add chicken, grapes and zucchini; toss to coat.

2. Arrange lettuce on plate. Top with chicken mixture; sprinkle with almonds.
                Makes 4 servings

roasted rosemary chicken leg

blackened chicken salad

nutrients per serving:

includes 1 tablespoon Ranch Salad Dressing

Calories: 222
Carbohydrate: 17 g
Calories From Fat: 16%
Total Fat: 4 g
Saturated Fat: 1 g
Cholesterol: 69 mg
Sodium: 191 mg
Dietary Fiber: 5 g
Protein: 30 g

2 cups cubed sourdough or French bread
Nonstick cooking spray
1 tablespoon paprika
1 teaspoon onion powder
1 teaspoon garlic powder
½ teaspoon dried oregano leaves
½ teaspoon dried thyme leaves
½ teaspoon ground white pepper
½ teaspoon ground red pepper
½ teaspoon black pepper
1 pound boneless skinless chicken breasts
4 cups bite-size pieces fresh spinach leaves
2 cups bite-size pieces romaine lettuce
2 cups cubed zucchini
2 cups cubed seeded cucumber
½ cup sliced green onions with tops
1 medium tomato, cut into 8 wedges
Ranch Salad Dressing (page 154)

1. Preheat oven to 375°F. To make croutons, spray bread cubes lightly with cooking spray; place in 15×10-inch jelly-roll pan. Bake 10 to 15 minutes or until browned, stirring occasionally. Set aside.

2. Combine paprika, onion powder, garlic powder, oregano, thyme, white pepper, red pepper and black pepper in small bowl; rub on all surfaces of chicken. Broil chicken, 6 inches from heat source, 7 to 8 minutes on each side or until chicken is no longer pink in center. Or, grill chicken, on covered grill over medium-hot coals, 10 minutes on each side or until chicken is no longer pink in center. Cool slightly. Cut chicken into thin strips.

3. Combine warm chicken, greens, zucchini, cucumber, green onions, tomato and reserved croutons in large bowl. Drizzle with Ranch Salad Dressing; toss to coat. Serve immediately.

Makes 4 servings

Tip: If you eliminate the croutons from this salad, the grams of carbohydrate will drop to 6 grams per serving.

blackened chicken salad

sirloin with sweet caramelized onions

Nonstick cooking spray
1 medium onion, very thinly sliced
1 boneless beef top sirloin steak (about 1 pound)
¼ cup water
2 tablespoons Worcestershire sauce
1 tablespoon sugar

1. Lightly coat 12-inch skillet with cooking spray; heat over high heat until hot. Add onion; cook and stir 4 minutes or until browned. Remove from skillet and set aside. Wipe out skillet with paper towel.

2. Coat same skillet with cooking spray; heat until hot. Add beef; cook 10 to 13 minutes for medium-rare to medium, turning once. Remove from heat and transfer to cutting board; let stand 3 minutes before slicing.

3. Meanwhile, return skillet to high heat until hot; add onion, water, Worcestershire sauce and sugar. Cook 30 to 45 seconds or until most liquid has evaporated.

4. Thinly slice beef on the diagonal and serve with onions. *Makes 4 servings*

ranch salad dressing

¼ cup water
3 tablespoons reduced-fat cucumber-ranch salad dressing
1 tablespoon reduced-fat mayonnaise or salad dressing
1 tablespoon lemon juice
2 teaspoons finely chopped parsley
⅛ teaspoon salt
⅛ teaspoon black pepper

Combine all ingredients in small jar with tight-fitting lid; shake well. Refrigerate until ready to use; shake before using. *Makes about ½ cup*

sirloin with sweet caramelized onions

grilled tilapia with zesty mustard sauce

Nonstick cooking spray
2 tablespoons light tub margarine
1 teaspoon Dijon mustard
½ teaspoon grated lemon peel
½ teaspoon Worcestershire sauce (lowest sodium available)
¼ teaspoon black pepper
½ teaspoon salt, divided
4 mild thin fish fillets, such as tilapia (about 4 ounces each)
1 ½ teaspoons paprika
½ medium lemon, cut into quarters
2 tablespoons finely chopped fresh parsley

1. Prepare grill for direct grilling. Lightly spray grill basket with cooking spray.

2. Combine margarine, mustard, lemon peel, Worcestershire sauce, pepper, and ¼ teaspoon salt in small bowl until well blended.

3. Rinse fish; pat dry with paper towels. Sprinkle both sides of fish with paprika and remaining ¼ teaspoon salt. Place fish in grill basket.

4. Grill fish, covered, over high heat 3 minutes. Turn and grill, covered, 2 to 3 minutes or until fish begins to flake when tested with fork.

5. Squeeze one lemon wedge over each fillet. Spoon mustard sauce over fish, spreading evenly with back of spoon. Sprinkle with parsley.   *Makes 4 servings*

grilled tilapia with zesty mustard sauce

blue cheese-stuffed sirloin patties

1½ pounds ground beef sirloin
½ cup (2 ounces) shredded sharp Cheddar cheese
¼ cup crumbled blue cheese
¼ cup finely chopped parsley
2 teaspoons Dijon mustard
1 teaspoon Worcestershire sauce
1 clove garlic, minced
¼ teaspoon salt
2 teaspoons olive oil
1 medium red bell pepper, cut into thin strips

1. Shape beef into 8 patties, about 4 inches in diameter and ¼ inch thick.

2. Combine cheeses, parsley, mustard, Worcestershire sauce, garlic and salt in small bowl; toss gently to blend.

3. Mound ¼ cheese mixture on each of 4 patties (about 3 tablespoons per patty). Top with remaining 4 patties; pinch edges of patties to seal completely. Set aside.

4. Heat oil in 12-inch nonstick skillet over medium-high heat until hot. Add pepper strips; cook and stir until edges of peppers begin to brown. Sprinkle with salt. Remove from skillet and keep warm.

5. Add beef patties to same skillet; cook on medium-high 5 minutes. Turn patties; top with peppers. Cook 4 minutes or until patties are no longer pink in centers (160°F).

Makes 4 servings

blue cheese-stuffed sirloin patty

vermouth salmon

nutrients per serving:

1 fillet

Calories: 162
Carbohydrate: <1 g
Calories From Fat: 49%
Total Fat: 9 g
Saturated Fat: 2 g
Cholesterol: 56 mg
Sodium: 41 mg
Dietary Fiber: <1 g
Protein: 17 g

2 (10×10-inch) sheets of heavy-duty foil
2 salmon fillets or steaks (3 ounces each)
   Pinch of salt and black pepper
4 sprigs fresh dill
2 slices lemon
1 tablespoon vermouth

1. Preheat oven to 375°F. Turn up the edges of 1 sheet of foil so juices will not run out. Place salmon in the center of the foil. Sprinkle with salt and pepper. Place dill on top of salmon and lemon slices on top of the dill. Pour vermouth evenly over fish pieces.

2. Cover fish with second sheet of foil. Crimp edges of foil together to seal packet. Place packet on baking sheet. Bake 20 to 25 minutes or until salmon flakes easily when tested with fork. *Makes 2 servings*

grilled chicken with chimichurri salsa

nutrients per serving:

Calories: 577
Carbohydrate: 3 g
Calories From Fat: 73%
Total Fat: 46 g
Saturated Fat: 8 g
Cholesterol: 108 mg
Sodium: 382 mg
Dietary Fiber: <1 g
Protein: 36 g

4 boneless skinless chicken breasts (6 ounces each)
½ cup plus 4 teaspoons olive oil
   Salt and black pepper
½ cup finely chopped parsley
¼ cup white wine vinegar
2 tablespoons finely chopped onion
3 cloves garlic, minced
1 fresh or canned jalapeño pepper, finely chopped
2 teaspoons dried oregano leaves

1. Prepare grill for direct grilling.

2. Brush chicken with 4 teaspoons olive oil; season with salt and black pepper. Place on oiled grid. Grill, covered, over medium heat 5 to 8 minutes on each side or until chicken is no longer pink in center.

3. To prepare sauce, combine parsley, vinegar, onion, garlic, jalapeño pepper, oregano, ½ cup olive oil, and salt and pepper to taste. Serve over chicken.
Makes 4 servings

Tip: Chimichurri salsa has a fresh, green color. Serve it with grilled steak or fish as well as chicken.

vermouth salmon

nutrients per serving:

Calories: 371
Carbohydrate: 7 g
Calories From Fat: 57%
Total Fat: 23 g
Saturated Fat: 9 g
Cholesterol: 105 mg
Sodium: 854 mg
Dietary Fiber: <1 g
Protein: 33 g

spinach, cheese and prosciutto-stuffed chicken breasts

4 boneless skinless chicken breasts (about 4 ounces each)
   Salt and black pepper
4 slices (½ ounce each) prosciutto*
4 slices (½ ounce each) smoked provolone
1 cup spinach leaves, chopped
4 tablespoons all-purpose flour, divided
1 tablespoon olive oil
1 tablespoon butter
1 cup chicken broth
1 tablespoon heavy cream

*Prosciutto, an Italian ham, is seasoned, cured and air-dried, not smoked. Look for imported or less expensive domestic prosciutto in delis and Italian food markets.

1. Preheat oven to 350°F.

2. To form pocket, cut each chicken breast horizontally almost to opposite edge. Fold back top half of chicken breast; sprinkle chicken lightly with salt and pepper. Place 1 slice prosciutto, 1 slice provolone and ¼ cup spinach on each chicken breast. Fold top half of breasts over filling.

3. Spread 3 tablespoons flour on plate. Holding chicken breast closed, coat with flour; shake off excess. Lightly sprinkle chicken with salt and pepper.

4. Heat oil and butter in large skillet over medium heat. Place chicken in skillet; cook about 4 minutes on each side or until browned.

5. Transfer chicken to shallow baking dish. Bake in oven 10 minutes or until chicken is no longer pink in center and juices run clear.

6. Whisk chicken broth and cream into remaining 1 tablespoon flour in small bowl. Pour chicken broth mixture into same skillet; heat over medium heat, stirring constantly, until sauce thickens, about 3 minutes. Spoon sauce onto serving plates; top with chicken breasts. *Makes 4 servings*

Tip: Swiss, Gruyère or mozzarella cheese may be substituted for the smoked provolone. Thinly sliced deli ham may be substituted for the prosciutto.

spinach, cheese and prosciutto-stuffed chicken breast

nutrients per serving:

Calories: 159
Carbohydrate: 7 g
Calories From Fat: 28%
Total Fat: 5 g
Saturated Fat: 5 g
Cholesterol: 43 mg
Sodium: 356 mg
Dietary Fiber: <1 g
Protein: 20 g

stir-fry beef & vegetable soup

1 boneless beef top sirloin or top round steak (about 1 pound)
2 teaspoons dark sesame oil, divided
3 cans (about 14 ounces each) reduced-sodium beef broth
1 package (16 ounces) frozen stir-fry vegetables
3 green onions, thinly sliced
¼ cup stir-fry sauce

1. Slice beef lengthwise in half, then crosswise into ⅛-inch-thick strips.

2. Heat Dutch oven over high heat. Add 1 teaspoon sesame oil and tilt pan to coat bottom. Add half the beef in single layer; cook 1 minute, without stirring, until slightly browned on bottom. Turn and brown other side about 1 minute. Remove beef from pan; set aside. Repeat with remaining 1 teaspoon sesame oil and beef; set aside.

3. Add broth to Dutch oven; cover and bring to a boil over high heat. Add vegetables; reduce heat and simmer 3 to 5 minutes or until vegetables are heated through. Add beef, green onions and stir-fry sauce; simmer 1 minute.

Makes 6 servings

Prep and Cook Time: 22 minutes

stir-fry beef & vegetable soup

nutrients per serving:

⅙ of total recipe

Calories: 162
Carbohydrate: 12 g
Calories From Fat: 17%
Total Fat: 3 g
Saturated Fat: <1 g
Cholesterol: 129 mg
Sodium: 678 mg
Dietary Fiber: 2 g
Protein: 21 g

mediterranean shrimp soup

2 cans (14½ ounces each) reduced-sodium chicken broth
1 can (14½ ounces) whole tomatoes, undrained and coarsely chopped
1 can (8 ounces) tomato sauce
1 medium onion, chopped
½ medium green bell pepper, chopped
½ cup orange juice
½ cup dry white wine (optional)
1 jar (2½ ounces) sliced mushrooms
¼ cup ripe olives, sliced
2 cloves garlic, minced
1 teaspoon dried basil leaves
2 bay leaves
¼ teaspoon fennel seeds, crushed
⅛ teaspoon black pepper
1 pound medium shrimp, peeled

Slow Cooker Directions

Place all ingredients except shrimp in slow cooker. Cover and cook on LOW 4 to 4½ hours or until vegetables are crisp-tender. Stir in shrimp. Cover; cook 15 to 30 minutes or until shrimp are opaque. Remove and discard bay leaves.

Makes 6 servings

Note: For a heartier soup, add some fish. Cut 1 pound of whitefish or cod into 1-inch pieces. Add the fish to the slow cooker 45 minutes before serving. Cover and cook on LOW.

mediterranean shrimp soup

nutrients per serving:

Calories: 267
Carbohydrate: 7 g
Calories From Fat: 51%
Total Fat: 15 g
Saturated Fat: 10 g
Cholesterol: 69 mg
Sodium: 308 mg
Dietary Fiber: 5 g
Protein: 28 g

pork curry over cauliflower couscous

3 tablespoons olive oil, divided
2 tablespoons mild curry powder
2 teaspoons prepared crushed garlic
1 ½ pounds pork (boneless shoulder, loin or chops), cubed
1 red or green bell pepper, seeded and diced
1 tablespoon cider vinegar
½ teaspoon salt
2 cups water
1 large head cauliflower

1. Heat 2 tablespoons oil over medium heat in large saucepan. Add curry powder and garlic; cook and stir 1 to 2 minutes until garlic is golden.

2. Add pork; stir to coat completely with curry and garlic. Cook and stir 5 to 7 minutes or until pork cubes are barely pink in center. Add bell pepper and vinegar; cook and stir 3 minutes or until bell pepper is soft. Sprinkle with salt.

3. Add water; bring to a boil. Reduce heat and simmer 30 to 45 minutes, stirring occasionally, until liquid is reduced and pork is tender, adding additional water as needed.

4. Meanwhile, trim and core cauliflower; cut into equal pieces. Place in food processor fitted with metal blade. Process using on/off pulsing action until cauliflower is in small uniform pieces about the size of cooked couscous. *Do not purée.*

5. Heat remaining 1 tablespoon oil over medium heat in 12-inch nonstick skillet. Add cauliflower; cook and stir 5 minutes or until cooked crisp-tender. *Do not overcook.* Serve pork curry over cauliflower. *Makes 6 servings*

pork curry over cauliflower couscous

crustless southwestern quiche

nutrients per serving:

Calories: 583
Carbohydrate: 9 g
Calories From Fat: 69%
Total Fat: 45 g
Saturated Fat: 18 g
Cholesterol: 516 mg
Sodium: 922 mg
Dietary Fiber: 2 g
Protein: 36 g

8 ounces chorizo sausage*
8 eggs
1 package (10 ounces) frozen chopped spinach, thawed and
squeezed dry
1 cup crumbled queso fresco or 1 cup (4 ounces) shredded Cheddar
or pepper Jack cheese
½ cup whipping cream or half-and-half
¼ cup salsa

*Chorizo, a spicy Mexican pork sausage, is flavored with garlic and chilies. It is available in most supermarkets. If it is not available, substitute 8 ounces bulk pork sausage plus ¼ teaspoon cayenne pepper.

1. Preheat oven to 400°F. Butter 10-inch quiche dish or deep-dish pie plate.

2. Remove sausage from casings. Crumble sausage into medium skillet. Cook over medium heat until sausage is browned, stirring to break up meat. Remove from heat; pour off drippings. Cool 5 minutes.

3. Beat eggs in medium bowl. Add spinach, cheese, cream and sausage; mix well. Pour into prepared quiche dish. Bake 20 minutes or until center is set. Let stand 5 minutes before cutting into wedges. Serve with salsa. *Makes 4 servings*

crustless southwestern quiche

tex-mex pork kabobs with chili sour cream sauce

2¼ teaspoons chili powder, divided
1¾ teaspoons ground cumin, divided
¾ teaspoon garlic powder, divided
¾ teaspoon onion powder, divided
¾ teaspoon dried oregano, divided
1 pork tenderloin (1½ pounds), trimmed and cut into 1-inch pieces
1 cup reduced-fat sour cream
¾ teaspoon salt, divided
¼ teaspoon black pepper
1 large red bell pepper, cut into small chunks
1 large green bell pepper, cut into small chunks
1 large yellow bell pepper, cut into small chunks

1. Combine 1½ teaspoons chili powder, 1 teaspoon cumin, ½ teaspoon garlic powder, ½ teaspoon onion powder and ½ teaspoon oregano in medium bowl. Add pork; toss until well coated. Cover tightly; refrigerate 2 to 3 hours.

2. Combine sour cream, ¼ teaspoon salt, black pepper and remaining ¾ teaspoon chili powder, ¾ teaspoon cumin, ¼ teaspoon garlic powder, ¼ teaspoon onion powder and ¼ teaspoon oregano in small bowl; mix well. Cover tightly; refrigerate 2 to 3 hours.

3. If using wooden skewers, soak in water 20 minutes before using. Prepare grill for direct cooking or preheat broiler.

4. Toss pork with remaining ½ teaspoon salt. Thread pork and bell peppers alternately onto 4 to 8 skewers.Grill skewers over medium-high heat 10 minutes or until pork is barely pink in center, turning several times. If broiling, place skewers on foil-lined baking sheet. Broil 8 inches from heat 5 minutes per side until barely pink in center, turning once. Serve immediately with sour cream sauce. *Makes 4 servings*

braciola

1 can (28 ounces) tomato sauce
2½ teaspoons dried oregano leaves, divided
1¼ teaspoons dried basil leaves, divided
1 teaspoon salt
½ pound bulk hot Italian sausage
½ cup chopped onion
¼ cup grated Parmesan cheese
2 cloves garlic, minced
1 tablespoon dried parsley flakes
1 to 2 beef flank steaks (about 2½ pounds)

nutrients per serving:

Calories: 349
Carbohydrate: 9 g
Calories From Fat: 44%
Total Fat: 17 g
Saturated Fat: 10 g
Cholesterol: 78 mg
Sodium: 1182 mg
Dietary Fiber: 2 g
Protein: 38 g

Slow Cooker Directions

1. Combine tomato sauce, 2 teaspoons oregano, 1 teaspoon basil and salt in medium bowl; set aside.

2. Cook sausage in large nonstick skillet over medium-high heat until no longer pink stirring to separate; drain well. Combine sausage, onion, cheese, garlic, parsley, remaining ½ teaspoon oregano and ¼ teaspoon basil in medium bowl; set aside.

3. Place steak on countertop between two pieces waxed paper. Pound with meat mallet until steak is ⅛ to ¼ inch thick. Cut steak into about 3-inch wide strips.

4. Spoon sausage mixture evenly onto each steak strip. Roll up, jelly-roll style, securing meat with toothpicks. Place each roll in slow cooker. Pour tomato sauce mixture over meat. Cover; cook on LOW 6 to 8 hours.

5. Cut each roll into slices. Arrange slices on dinner plates. Top with hot tomato sauce.
Makes 8 servings

Prep Time: 35 minutes
Cook Time: 6 to 8 hours

chicken teriyaki

nutrients per serving:

Calories: 224
Carbohydrate: 5 g
Calories From Fat: 32%
Total Fat: 8 g
Saturated Fat: 1 g
Cholesterol: 82 mg
Sodium: 1003 mg
Dietary Fiber: <1 g
Protein: 26 g

8 large chicken drumsticks (about 2 pounds)
⅓ cup teriyaki sauce
2 tablespoons brandy or apple juice
1 green onion, minced
1 tablespoon vegetable oil
1 teaspoon ground ginger
½ teaspoon sugar
¼ teaspoon garlic powder
Prepared sweet and sour sauce (optional)

1. Remove skin from drumsticks, if desired, by pulling skin toward end of leg using paper towel; discard skin.

2. Place chicken in large resealable plastic food storage bag. Combine teriyaki sauce, brandy, onion, oil, ginger, sugar and garlic powder in small bowl; pour over chicken. Close bag securely, turning to coat. Marinate in refrigerator at least 1 hour or overnight, turning occasionally.

3. Prepare grill for indirect cooking.

4. Drain chicken; reserve marinade. Place chicken on grid directly over drip pan. Grill, covered, over medium-high heat 60 minutes or until chicken is no longer pink in center and juices run clear, turning and brushing with reserved marinade every 20 minutes. *Do not brush with marinade during last 5 minutes of grilling.* Discard remaining marinade. Serve with sweet and sour sauce, if desired.

Makes 4 servings

chicken teriyaki

nutrients per serving:

Calories: 135
Carbohydrate: 6 g
Calories From Fat: 21%
Total Fat: 3 g
Saturated Fat: 1 g
Cholesterol: 46 mg
Sodium: 307 mg
Dietary Fiber: 2 g
Protein: 19 g

asian chicken kabobs

1 pound boneless skinless chicken breasts
2 small zucchini or yellow squash, cut into 1-inch slices
8 large fresh mushrooms
1 cup red, yellow or green bell pepper pieces
2 tablespoons reduced-sodium soy sauce
2 tablespoons dry sherry
1 teaspoon dark sesame oil
2 cloves garlic, minced
2 large green onions, cut into 1-inch pieces

1. Cut chicken into 1½-inch pieces; place in large plastic bag. Add zucchini, mushrooms and bell pepper to bag. Combine soy sauce, sherry, oil and garlic in cup; pour over chicken and vegetables. Close bag securely; turn to coat. Marinate in refrigerator at least 30 minutes or up to 4 hours.

2. Soak 4 (12-inch) skewers in water to cover 20 minutes.

3. Drain chicken and vegetables; reserve marinade. Alternately thread chicken and vegetables with onions onto skewers.

4. Place on rack of broiler pan. Brush with half of reserved marinade. Broil 5 to 6 inches from heat 5 minutes. Turn kabobs over; brush with remaining marinade. Broil 5 minutes or until chicken is no longer pink. Garnish with green onion brushes, if desired.

Makes 4 servings

asian chicken kabobs

nutrients per serving:

Calories: 304
Carbohydrate: 18 g
Calories From Fat: 30%
Total Fat: 10 g
Saturated Fat: 3 g
Cholesterol: 67 mg
Sodium: 836 mg
Dietary Fiber: 3 g
Protein: 37 g

lime-poached fish with corn and chili salsa

4 swordfish steaks, 1 inch thick (about 1½ pounds)*
1 cup baby carrots, cut lengthwise into halves
2 green onions, cut into 1-inch pieces
3 tablespoons lime juice
½ teaspoon salt, divided
½ teaspoon chili powder
1½ cups chopped tomatoes
1 cup frozen corn, thawed
1 can (4 ounces) chopped green chilies, drained
2 tablespoons chopped fresh cilantro
1 tablespoon margarine or butter

*Tuna or halibut steaks can be substituted.

1. Place fish and carrots in saucepan just large enough to hold them in single layer. Add onions, lime juice, ¼ teaspoon salt and chili powder. Add enough water to just cover fish.

2. Bring to a simmer over medium heat. Cook 8 minutes or until center of fish begins to flake easily when tested with fork. Transfer to serving plates with spatula.

3. Meanwhile, to prepare salsa, combine tomatoes, corn, chilies, cilantro and remaining ¼ teaspoon salt in medium bowl; toss well.

4. Drain carrots; add margarine. Transfer to serving plates; serve with salsa.

Makes 4 servings

Tip: If time allows, prepare the salsa in advance so the flavors have more time to develop. Do not add salt until ready to serve. Cover and refrigerate salsa up to 1 day before serving.

Prep and Cook Time: 15 minutes

lime-poached fish with corn and chili salsa

nutrients per serving:

¼ of total recipe

Calories: 254
Carbohydrate: 6 g
Calories From Fat: 52%
Total Fat: 15 g
Saturated Fat: 3 g
Cholesterol: 66 mg
Sodium: 196 mg
Dietary Fiber: 2 g
Protein: 24 g

greek-style salmon

1½ teaspoons olive oil
1¾ cups diced tomatoes, drained
6 pitted black olives, coarsely chopped
4 pitted green olives, coarsely chopped
3 tablespoons lemon juice
2 tablespoons chopped fresh Italian parsley
1 tablespoon capers, rinsed and drained
2 cloves garlic, thinly sliced
¼ teaspoon black papper
1 pound salmon fillets

1. Heat oil in large skillet over medium-high heat. Add tomatoes, olives, lemon juice, parsley, capers, garlic and pepper; bring to a simmer over medium heat, stirring frequently.

2. Simmer tomato mixture 5 minutes or until reduced by about one-third, stirring occasionally.

3. Rinse salmon and pat dry with paper towels. Push sauce to one side of skillet. Add salmon to skillet; spoon tomato mixture over salmon.

4. Cover and cook 10 to 15 minutes or until salmon begins to flake when tested with fork.   *Makes 4 servings*

Note: Spanish-style, or green olives, are picked underripe, soaked in lye and then cured for six months or more. They have a tart, salty taste and are sold pitted, unpitted and stuffed with pimiento..

greek-style salmon

nutrients per serving:

Calories: 188
Carbohydrate: 15 g
Calories From Fat: 24%
Total Fat: 5 g
Saturated Fat: 1 g
Cholesterol: 54 mg
Sodium: 704 mg
Dietary Fiber: 2 g
Protein: 22 g

chicken and vegetable chowder

1 pound boneless skinless chicken breasts, cut into 1-inch pieces
10 ounces frozen broccoli cuts
1 cup sliced carrots
1 jar (4½ ounces) sliced mushrooms, drained
½ cup chopped onion
½ cup whole kernel corn
2 cloves garlic, minced
½ teaspoon dried thyme leaves
1 can (14½ ounces) reduced-sodium chicken broth
1 can (10¾ ounces) condensed cream of potato soup
⅓ cup half-and-half

Slow Cooker Directions

1. Combine all ingredients except half-and-half in slow cooker. Cover and cook on LOW 5 hours or until vegetables are tender and chicken is no longer pink in center.

2. Stir in half-and-half. Turn to HIGH. Cover and cook 15 minutes or until heated through. *Makes 6 servings*

Variation: If desired, add ½ cup (2 ounces) shredded Swiss or Cheddar cheese to thickened chowder, stirring over LOW heat until melted.

chicken and vegetable chowder

mexican tortilla soup

nutrients per serving:

1¾ cups soup with tortilla strips

Calories: 184
Carbohydrate: 16 g
Calories From Fat: 15%
Total Fat: 3 g
Saturated Fat: 1 g
Cholesterol: 58 mg
Sodium: 132 mg
Dietary Fiber: 4 g
Protein: 23 g

Nonstick cooking spray
2 pounds boneless skinless chicken breasts, cut into ½-inch strips
4 cups diced carrots
2 cups sliced celery
1 cup chopped green bell pepper
1 cup chopped onion
4 cloves garlic, minced
1 jalapeño pepper,* seeded and sliced
1 teaspoon dried oregano leaves
½ teaspoon ground cumin
8 cups fat-free reduced-sodium chicken broth
1 large tomato, seeded and chopped
4 to 5 tablespoons lime juice
2 (6-inch) corn tortillas, cut into ¼-inch strips
Salt (optional)
3 tablespoons finely chopped fresh cilantro

Jalapeño peppers can sting and irritate the skin; wear rubber gloves when handling peppers and do not touch eyes. Wash hands after handling.

1. Preheat oven to 350°F. Spray large nonstick Dutch oven with cooking spray; heat over medium heat. Add chicken; cook and stir about 10 minutes or until browned and no longer pink in center. Add carrots, celery, bell pepper, onion, garlic, jalapeño pepper, oregano and cumin; cook and stir over medium heat 5 minutes.

2. Stir in chicken broth, tomato and lime juice; heat to a boil. Reduce heat to low; cover and simmer 15 to 20 minutes.

3. Meanwhile, spray tortilla strips lightly with cooking spray; sprinkle very lightly with salt, if desired. Place on baking sheet. Bake about 10 minutes or until browned and crisp, stirring occasionally.

4. Stir cilantro into soup. Ladle soup into bowls; top evenly with tortilla strips.

Makes 8 servings

mexican tortilla soup

sensational side dishes

jalapeño wild rice cakes

nutrients per serving:

1 (3-inch diameter) rice cake

Calories: 63
Carbohydrate: 5 g
Calories From Fat: 57%
Total Fat: 4 g
Saturated Fat: 1 g
Cholesterol: 27 mg
Sodium: 330 mg
Dietary Fiber: <1 g
Protein: 2 g

⅓ cup wild rice
¾ cup water
½ teaspoon salt, divided
1 tablespoon all-purpose flour
½ teaspoon baking powder
1 egg
1 jalapeño pepper,* finely chopped
2 tablespoons minced onion
1 tablespoon freshly grated ginger *or* 2 teaspoons ground ginger
2 tablespoons vegetable or olive oil

Jalapeño peppers can sting and irritate the skin; wear rubber gloves when handling peppers and do not touch eyes. Wash hands after handling.

1. Combine rice, water and ¼ teaspoon salt in medium saucepan. Bring to a boil. Reduce heat; cover and simmer 40 to 45 minutes or until rice is tender. Drain rice, if necessary; place in medium bowl. Add flour, baking powder and remaining ¼ teaspoon salt; mix until blended.

2. Whisk egg, jalapeño pepper, onion and ginger together in small bowl. Pour egg mixture over rice; mix until well blended.

3. Heat oil in large nonstick skillet over medium heat. Spoon 2 tablespoons rice mixture into pan and shape into cake. Cook, 4 cakes at a time, 3 minutes on each side or until golden brown. Transfer to paper towels. Serve immediately or refrigerate rice cakes for up to 24 hours. *Makes 8 (3-inch diameter) rice cakes*

Tip: To reheat cold rice cakes, preheat oven to 400°F. Place rice cakes in single layer on baking sheet; heat 5 minutes.

jalapeño wild rice cakes

nutrients per serving:

Calories: 19
Carbohydrate: 5 g
Calories From Fat: 7%
Total Fat: <1 g
Saturated Fat: <1 g
Cholesterol: 0 mg
Sodium: 2 mg
Dietary Fiber: 1 g
Protein: <1 g

strawberry blueberry salsa

¾ cup chopped strawberries
⅓ cup chopped blueberries
2 tablespoons chopped green bell pepper
2 tablespoons chopped carrot
1 tablespoon chopped onion
2 teaspoons cider vinegar
1 teaspoon minced jalapeño pepper*
⅛ teaspoon ground ginger

*Jalapeño peppers can sting and irritate the skin; wear rubber gloves when handling peppers and do not touch eyes. Wash hands after handling.

Combine all ingredients in small bowl. Let stand 20 minutes to allow flavors to blend. Serve with grilled chicken, pork or fish. *Makes 4 servings*

nutrients per serving:

Calories: 28
Carbohydrate: 7 g
Calories From Fat: 6%
Total Fat: <1 g
Saturated Fat: 0 g
Cholesterol: 0 mg
Sodium: 189 mg
Dietary Fiber: 2 g
Protein: 1 g

lemony cabbage slaw with curry

4 cups shredded green or white cabbage
2 tablespoons chopped green bell pepper
2 tablespoons chopped red bell pepper
1 green onion, thinly sliced
2 tablespoons cider vinegar
1 tablespoon lemon juice
1 tablespoon sugar
1 teaspoon curry powder
½ teaspoon salt
½ teaspoon celery seeds
Green and red bell pepper rings for garnish

1. Mix cabbage, bell peppers and green onion in large bowl. Combine vinegar, lemon juice, sugar, curry powder, salt and celery seeds in small bowl. Pour over cabbage mixture; mix well.

2. Refrigerate, covered, at least 4 hours or overnight, stirring occasionally. Garnish with bell pepper rings. *Makes 6 servings*

strawberry blueberry salsa

sun-dried tomato scones

2 cups buttermilk baking mix
¼ cup (1 ounce) grated Parmesan cheese
1½ teaspoons dried basil
⅔ cup reduced-fat (2%) milk
½ cup chopped drained oil-packed sun-dried tomatoes
¼ cup chopped green onions

1. Preheat oven to 450°F. Combine baking mix, cheese and basil in medium bowl.

2. Stir in milk, tomatoes and onions. Mix just until dry ingredients are moistened. Drop by heaping teaspoonfuls onto greased baking sheet.

3. Bake 8 to 10 minutes or until light golden brown. Remove baking sheet to cooling rack; let stand 5 minutes. Remove scones and serve warm or at room temperature.

Makes 1½ dozen scones

Prep and Cook Time: 20 minutes

red and greens salad

2 tablespoons raspberry vinegar
1 teaspoon white pepper
1 teaspoon sugar
¼ teaspoon salt
2 tablespoons olive or canola oil
1 bag (4 to 6 ounces) mixed baby salad greens
1 carton (6 ounces) fresh raspberries

1. To prepare dressing, whisk together vinegar, pepper, sugar and salt in small bowl until salt and sugar dissolve. Add oil and whisk to blend. Reserve.

2. Place greens in large salad bowl. Add reserved dressing and toss gently to coat greens. Add raspberries and toss gently to mix and coat with dressing. Divide salad evenly among 8 plates.

Makes 8 servings

Tip: As raspberries are gently tossed, they will release a little of their juice and enhance the flavor of the dressing.

sun-dried tomato scones

nutrients per serving:

Calories: 49
Carbohydrate: 9 g
Calories From Fat: 23%
Total Fat: 1 g
Saturated Fat: <1 g
Cholesterol: 0 mg
Sodium: 71 mg
Dietary Fiber: 3 g
Protein: 1 g

tabbouleh

½ cup uncooked bulgur wheat
¾ cup boiling water
¼ teaspoon salt
5 teaspoons lemon juice
2 teaspoons olive oil
½ teaspoon dried basil leaves
¼ teaspoon black pepper
1 green onion, thinly sliced
½ cup chopped cucumber
½ cup chopped green bell pepper
½ cup chopped tomato
¼ cup chopped fresh parsley
2 teaspoons chopped mint (optional)

1. Rinse bulgur thoroughly in colander under cold water, picking out any debris. Drain well; transfer to medium heatproof bowl. Stir in boiling water and salt. Cover; let stand 30 minutes. Drain well.

2. Combine lemon juice, oil, basil and black pepper in small bowl. Pour over bulgur; mix well.

3. Layer bulgur, onion, cucumber, bell pepper and tomato in clear glass bowl; sprinkle with parsley and mint, if desired.

4. Refrigerate, covered, at least 2 hours to allow flavors to blend. Serve layered or toss before serving.
Makes 8 servings

broccoli italian style

1¼ pounds broccoli
2 tablespoons lemon juice
1 teaspoon olive oil
1 clove garlic, minced
1 teaspoon chopped fresh parsley
Dash pepper

1. Trim broccoli, discarding tough part of stems. Cut broccoli into florets with 2-inch stems. Peel remaining broccoli stems; cut into ½-inch-thick slices.

2. Bring 1 quart water to a boil in large saucepan over high heat. Add broccoli; return to a boil. Reduce heat to medium-high. Cook, uncovered, 3 to 5 minutes or until broccoli is fork-tender. Drain; arrange evenly in serving dish.

3. Combine lemon juice, oil, garlic, parsley and pepper in small bowl. Pour over broccoli, turning to coat. Let stand, covered, 1 to 2 hours before serving to allow flavors to blend. *Makes 4 servings*

nutrients per serving:

Calories: 44
Carbohydrate: 7 g
Calories From Fat: 26%
Total Fat: 2 g
Saturated Fat: <1 g
Cholesterol: 0 mg
Sodium: 29 mg
Dietary Fiber: 3 g
Protein: 3 g

oven-roasted asparagus

1 bunch (12 to 14 ounces) asparagus spears
1 tablespoon olive oil
½ teaspoon salt
¼ teaspoon ground black pepper
¼ cup shredded Asiago or Parmesan cheese

1. Preheat oven to 425°F.

2. Trim off and discard tough ends of asparagus spears. Peel stem ends of asparagus with vegetable peeler, if desired. Arrange asparagus in shallow baking dish. Drizzle oil onto asparagus; turn stalks to coat. Sprinkle with salt and pepper.

3. Bake until asparagus is tender, about 12 to 18 minutes depending on thickness of asparagus. Chop or leave spears whole. Sprinkle with cheese. *Makes 4 servings*

nutrients per serving:

Calories: 75
Carbohydrate: 4 g
Calories From Fat: 60%
Total Fat: 5 g
Saturated Fat: 2 g
Cholesterol: 6 mg
Sodium: 286 mg
Dietary Fiber: 2 g
Protein: 4 g

grilled vegetables

nutrients per serving:

Calories: 34
Carbohydrate: 8 g
Calories From Fat: 6%
Total Fat: <1 g
Saturated Fat: <1 g
Cholesterol: 0 mg
Sodium: 190 mg
Dietary Fiber: 2 g
Protein: 1 g

¼ cup minced fresh herbs, such as parsley, thyme, rosemary, oregano or basil
1 small eggplant (about ¾ pound), cut into ¼-inch-thick slices
½ teaspoon salt
 Nonstick cooking spray
1 each red, green and yellow bell pepper, quartered and seeded
2 zucchini, cut lengthwise into ¼-inch-thick slices
1 fennel bulb, cut lengthwise into ¼-inch-thick slices

1. Combine herbs in small bowl; let stand 3 hours or overnight.

2. Place eggplant in large colander over bowl; sprinkle with salt. Drain 1 hour.

3. Heat grill until coals are glowing red. Spray vegetables with cooking spray and sprinkle with herb mixture. Grill 10 to 15 minutes or until fork-tender and lightly browned on both sides. (Cooking times vary depending on vegetable; remove vegetables as they are done to avoid overcooking.) *Makes 6 servings*

stilton salad dressing

nutrients per serving:

Calories: 51
Carbohydrate: 2 g
Calories From Fat: 55%
Total Fat: 3 g
Saturated Fat: 2 g
Cholesterol: 8 mg
Sodium: 265 mg
Dietary Fiber: <1 g
Protein: 4 g

½ cup buttermilk
¼ cup silken firm tofu
 2 ounces Stilton cheese
 1 teaspoon lemon juice
 1 clove garlic, peeled
¼ teaspoon salt
⅛ teaspoon black pepper
 2 tablespoons low-fat (1%) cottage cheese
 Romaine lettuce hearts, torn into bite-size pieces (optional)
 Toasted chopped walnuts (optional)

1. Place buttermilk, tofu, Stilton cheese, lemon juice, garlic, salt and pepper in blender or food processor; process until smooth. Pour mixture into small bowl; fold in cottage cheese.

2. Store in airtight container and refrigerate 3 hours or overnight before serving. Serve with romaine lettuce and toasted walnuts, if desired. *Makes 6 servings*

grilled vegetables

buttermilk-herb dressing

½ cup plus 1 tablespoon nonfat buttermilk
3 tablespoons raspberry-flavored vinegar
1 tablespoon chopped fresh basil leaves
1½ teaspoons snipped fresh chives
¼ teaspoon minced garlic

Place all ingredients in small bowl; stir to combine. Store, covered, in refrigerator up to 2 days. *Makes about ¾ cup*

autumn casserole

¼ cup fat-free reduced-sodium chicken broth or water
2 cups sliced mushrooms
2 cups chopped stemmed and washed fresh spinach
1 cup diced red bell pepper
1 clove garlic, minced
1 cup cooked spaghetti squash
¼ teaspoon salt
¼ teaspoon black pepper
⅛ teaspoon dried Italian seasoning
⅛ teaspoon red pepper flakes (optional)
¼ cup grated Parmesan cheese

1. Preheat oven to 350°F. Spray 1-quart casserole with nonstick cooking spray.

2. Heat chicken broth in medium saucepan. Add mushrooms, spinach, bell pepper and garlic. Cook 10 minutes or until vegetables are tender, stirring frequently. Stir in squash. Add salt, black pepper, Italian seasoning and red pepper flakes, if desired.

3. Spoon into prepared casserole. Sprinkle with cheese. Bake 5 to 10 minutes or until cheese melts. *Makes 6 servings*

Note: For 1 cup cooked spaghetti squash, place half small spaghetti squash in microwavable dish and add ¼ cup water. Microwave at HIGH 8 to 10 minutes or until squash is tender when pierced with a fork. Discard seeds and scrape out strands of squash. Or, bake in preheated 350°F oven 45 minutes or until tender.

buttermilk-herb dressing

nutrients per serving:

Calories: 72
Carbohydrate: 9 g
Calories From Fat: 45%
Total Fat: 4 g
Saturated Fat: <1 g
Cholesterol: 0 mg
Sodium: 163 mg
Dietary Fiber: 2 g
Protein: 2 g

marinated tomato salad

Marinade
1½ **cups tarragon or white wine vinegar**
 ½ **teaspoon salt**
 ¼ **cup finely chopped shallots**
 2 **tablespoons finely chopped chives**
 2 **tablespoons fresh lemon juice**
 ¼ **teaspoon white pepper**
 2 **tablespoons extra-virgin olive oil**

Salad
 6 **plum tomatoes, quartered vertically**
 2 **large yellow tomatoes,* sliced horizontally into ½-inch slices**
16 **red cherry tomatoes, halved vertically**
16 **small yellow pear tomatoes,* halved vertically**

Substitute 10 plum tomatoes, quartered vertically, for yellow tomatoes and yellow pear tomatoes, if desired.

1. To prepare marinade, combine vinegar and salt in large bowl; stir until salt is completely dissolved. Add shallots, chives, lemon juice and white pepper; mix well. Slowly whisk in oil until well blended.

2. Add tomatoes to marinade; toss well. Cover and let stand at room temperature 2 to 3 hours.

3. To serve, place 3 plum tomato quarters on each of 8 salad plates. Add 2 slices yellow tomato, 4 cherry tomato halves and 4 pear tomato halves. Garnish each plate with sunflower sprouts, if desired. (Or, place all marinated tomatoes on large serving plate.)
Makes 8 servings

marinated tomato salad

stir-fried asparagus

½ **pound asparagus**
1 **tablespoon olive or canola oil**
1 **cup celery slices**
½ **cup bottled roasted red peppers, drained and diced**
¼ **teaspoon black pepper**
¼ **cup sliced almonds, toasted***

To toast almonds, place in small dry skillet. Cook over medium heat, stirring constantly, until almonds are lightly browned.

1. Trim ends from asparagus; cut stalks diagonally into 1-inch pieces.

2. Heat oil in 12-inch nonstick skillet over medium-high heat. Add celery; stir-fry 2 minutes. Add asparagus and red peppers. Stir-fry 3 to 4 minutes or until asparagus is crisp tender.

3. Add black pepper and almonds; mix until blended.   *Makes 6 servings*

nutrients per serving:

Calories: 67
Carbohydrate: 4 g
Calories From Fat: 67%
Total Fat: 5 g
Saturated Fat: <1 g
Cholesterol: 0 mg
Sodium: 18 mg
Dietary Fiber: 2 g
Protein: 2 g

balsamic vinaigrette

¼ **cup balsamic vinegar**
¼ **cup water**
3 **tablespoons olive oil**
2 **tablespoons finely chopped red or green onion**
3 **cloves garlic, minced**
¾ **teaspoon dried chervil leaves**
½ **teaspoon celery seeds**

Combine all ingredients in jar with tight-fitting lid; refrigerate until serving time. Shake well before using.   *Makes about ⅔ cup*

nutrients per serving:

1 tablespoon

Calories: 38
Carbohydrate: 1 g
Calories From Fat: 87%
Total Fat: 4 g
Saturated Fat: 1 g
Cholesterol: 0 mg
Sodium: 1 mg
Dietary Fiber: <1 g
Protein: <1 g

stir-fried asparagus

broccoli with creamy lemon sauce

nutrients per serving:

Calories: 44
Carbohydrate: 7 g
Calories From Fat: 18%
Total Fat: 1 g
Saturated Fat: <1 g
Cholesterol: 4 mg
Sodium: 216 mg
Dietary Fiber: 2 g
Protein: 2 g

2 tablespoons fat-free mayonnaise
4½ teaspoons reduced-fat sour cream
1 tablespoon fat-free (skim) milk
1 to 1½ teaspoons lemon juice
⅛ teaspoon ground turmeric
1¼ cups hot cooked broccoli florets

Combine all ingredients except broccoli in top of double boiler. Cook over simmering water 5 minutes or until heated through, stirring constantly. Serve over hot cooked broccoli.   *Makes 2 servings*

vegetable napoleon

nutrients per serving:

Calories: 78
Carbohydrate: 9 g
Calories From Fat: 25%
Total Fat: 2 g
Saturated Fat: 1 g
Cholesterol: 6 mg
Sodium: 105 mg
Dietary Fiber: 3 g
Protein: 6 g

1 teaspoon salt-free garlic and herb seasoning mix
¼ teaspoon black pepper
¼ teaspoon garlic powder
1 large yellow squash, thinly sliced lengthwise
1 large zucchini, thinly sliced lengthwise
¼ cup (1 ounce) shredded reduced-fat mozzarella cheese
1 large tomato, thinly sliced*

For easier slicing, use a serrated bread knife to slice tomatoes.

1. Preheat oven to 350°F. Lightly spray small loaf pan with cooking spray. Combine seasoning mix, pepper and garlic powder, in small bowl.

2. Place one layer of squash and zucchini in bottom of loaf pan. Sprinkle with ⅓ of seasoning mixture and 1 tablespoon cheese. Layer tomato slices over squash. Top with ⅓ of seasoning mixture and 1 tablespoon of cheese. Top with remaining squash, seasoning mixture and cheese.

3. Bake 35 minutes or until vegetables are tender and cheese is melted. Remove from oven and cool slightly before slicing.   *Makes 2 servings*

broccoli with creamy lemon sauce

indian-style vegetable stir-fry

nutrients per serving:

⅙ of total recipe (without garnish)

Calories: 40
Carbohydrate: 7 g
Calories From Fat: 22%
Total Fat: 1 g
Saturated Fat: <1 g
Cholesterol: 0 mg
Sodium: 198 mg
Dietary Fiber: 1 g
Protein: 2 g

1 teaspoon canola oil
1 teaspoon curry powder
1 teaspoon ground cumin
⅛ teaspoon red pepper flakes
1½ teaspoons minced seeded jalapeño pepper*
2 cloves garlic, minced
¾ cup chopped red bell pepper
¾ cup thinly sliced carrots
3 cups cauliflower florets
½ cup water, divided
½ teaspoon salt
2 teaspoons finely chopped fresh cilantro (optional)

*Jalapeño peppers can sting and irritate the skin; wear rubber gloves when handling peppers and do not touch eyes. Wash hands after handling.

1. Heat oil in large nonstick skillet over medium-high heat. Add curry powder, cumin and red pepper flakes; cook and stir about 30 seconds.

2. Stir in jalapeño pepper and garlic. Add bell pepper and carrots; mix well. Add cauliflower; reduce heat to medium.

3. Stir in ¼ cup water; cook and stir until water evaporates. Add remaining ¼ cup water; cover and cook about 8 to 10 minutes or until vegetables are crisp-tender, stirring occasionally.

4. Add salt; mix well. Sprinkle with cilantro and garnish with mizuna and additional red bell pepper, if desired.   *Makes 6 servings*

indian-style vegetable stir-fry

super snacks

jerk wings with ranch dipping sauce

½ **cup mayonnaise**
½ **cup plain yogurt or sour cream**
1½ **teaspoons salt, divided**
1¼ **teaspoons garlic powder, divided**
½ **teaspoon black pepper, divided**
¼ **teaspoon onion powder**
2 **tablespoons orange juice**
1 **teaspoon sugar**
1 **teaspoon dried thyme leaves**
1 **teaspoon paprika**
¼ **teaspoon ground nutmeg**
¼ **teaspoon ground red pepper**
2½ **pounds chicken wings (about 10 wings)**

1. Preheat oven to 450°F. For Ranch Dipping Sauce, combine mayonnaise, yogurt, ½ teaspoon salt, ¼ teaspoon garlic powder, ¼ teaspoon black pepper and onion powder in small bowl.

2. Combine orange juice, sugar, thyme, paprika, nutmeg, red pepper, remaining 1 teaspoon salt, 1 teaspoon garlic powder and ¼ teaspoon black pepper in small bowl.

3. Cut tips from wings; discard. Place wings in large bowl. Drizzle with orange juice mixture; toss to coat.

4. Transfer chicken to greased broiler pan. Bake 25 to 30 minutes or until juices run clear and skin is crisp. Serve with Ranch Dipping Sauce.   *Makes 6 to 7 servings*

Serving Suggestion: Serve with celery sticks.

jerk wings with ranch dipping sauce

wild wedges

nutrients per serving:

2 wedges

Calories: 76
Carbohydrate: 8 g
Calories From Fat: 24%
Total Fat: 2 g
Saturated Fat: 1 g
Cholesterol: 14 mg
Sodium: 282 mg
Dietary Fiber: 4 g
Protein: 7 g

    2 (8-inch) fat-free flour tortillas
    Nonstick cooking spray
⅓ cup shredded reduced-fat Cheddar cheese
⅓ cup chopped cooked chicken or turkey
  1 green onion, thinly sliced
  2 tablespoons mild, thick and chunky salsa

1. Heat large nonstick skillet over medium heat until hot.

2. Spray one side of one flour tortilla with cooking spray; place, sprayed side down, in skillet. Top with cheese, chicken, green onion and salsa. Place remaining tortilla over mixture; spray with cooking spray.

3. Cook 2 to 3 minutes per side or until golden brown and cheese is melted. Cut into 8 triangles. *Makes 4 servings*

bacon & cheese dip

nutrients per serving:

2 tablespoons dip

Calories: 114
Carbohydrate: 2 g
Calories From Fat: 64%
Total Fat: 8 g
Saturated Fat: 4 g
Cholesterol: 27 mg
Sodium: 436 mg
Dietary Fiber: <1 g
Protein: 7 g

  2 packages (8 ounces each) reduced-fat cream cheese, softened,
    cut into cubes
  4 cups (16 ounces) shredded reduced-fat sharp Cheddar cheese
  1 cup evaporated skimmed milk
  2 tablespoons prepared mustard
  1 tablespoon chopped onion
  2 teaspoons Worcestershire sauce
½ teaspoon salt
¼ teaspoon hot pepper sauce
  1 pound turkey bacon, crisp-cooked and crumbled

Slow Cooker Directions

Place cream cheese, Cheddar cheese, evaporated milk, mustard, onion, Worcestershire sauce, salt and pepper sauce into slow cooker. Cover; cook, stirring occasionally, on LOW 1 hour or until cheese melts. Stir in bacon; adjust seasonings. Serve with fruit and vegetable dippers. *Makes about 4 cups*

wild wedges

roasted garlic spread with three cheeses

2 medium heads garlic
2 packages (8 ounces each) fat-free cream cheese, softened
1 package (3½ ounces) goat cheese
2 tablespoons (1 ounce) crumbled blue cheese
1 teaspoon dried thyme leaves

1. Preheat oven to 400°F. Cut tops off garlic heads to expose tops of cloves. Place garlic in small baking pan; bake 45 minutes or until garlic is very tender. Remove from pan; cool completely. Squeeze garlic into small bowl; mash with fork.

2. Beat cream cheese and goat cheese in small bowl until smooth; stir in blue cheese, garlic and thyme. Cover; refrigerate 3 hours or overnight. Spoon dip into serving bowl; serve with cucumbers, radishes, carrots or yellow bell peppers, if desired. Garnish with fresh thyme and red bell pepper strip, if desired.

Makes 21 servings

nutrients per serving:

2 tablespoons spread

Calories: 37
Carbohydrate: 2 g
Calories From Fat: 29%
Total Fat: 1 g
Saturated Fat: <1 g
Cholesterol: 9 mg
Sodium: 157 mg
Dietary Fiber: <1 g
Protein: 4 g

peaches and creamy dip with waffle wedges

4 ounces reduced-fat cream cheese
⅓ cup sugar-free peach preserves
1 tablespoon fat-free (skim) milk
2 packages sugar substitute
½ teaspoon vanilla
4 low-fat toaster waffles
Ground cinnamon to taste

1. Place all ingredients, except waffles and cinnamon, in blender and process until smooth. Set aside.

2. Toast waffles and cut each waffle into 6 wedges.

3. Place cream cheese mixture in small serving bowl and sprinkle with cinnamon. Serve with waffle wedges for dipping.

Makes 24 wedges and about ¾ cup cream cheese mixture

nutrients per serving:

1 wedge and about 2 teaspoons dip

Calories: 54
Carbohydrate: 5 g
Calories From Fat: 29%
Total Fat: 3 g
Saturated Fat: <1 g
Cholesterol: <1 mg
Sodium: 57 mg
Dietary Fiber: <1 g
Protein: 2 g

roasted garlic spread with three cheeses

angelic deviled eggs

6 eggs
¼ cup low-fat (1%) cottage cheese
3 tablespoons prepared fat-free ranch dressing
2 teaspoons Dijon mustard
2 tablespoons minced fresh chives or dill
1 tablespoon diced well-drained pimiento or roasted red pepper

1. Place eggs in medium saucepan; add enough water to cover. Bring to a boil over medium heat. Remove from heat; cover. Let stand 15 minutes. Drain. Add cold water to eggs in saucepan; let stand until eggs are cool. Drain. Remove shells from eggs.

2. Cut eggs lengthwise in half. Remove yolks, reserving 3 yolk halves. Discard remaining yolks or reserve for another use. Place egg whites, cut sides up, on serving plate; cover with plastic wrap. Refrigerate while preparing filling.

3. Combine cottage cheese, dressing, mustard and reserved yolk halves in mini food processor; process until smooth. (Or, place in small bowl and mash with fork until well blended.) Transfer cheese mixture to small bowl; stir in chives and pimiento. Spoon into egg whites. Cover and chill at least 1 hour. Garnish, if desired.

Makes 12 servings

nutrients per serving:

2 filled egg halves (without garnish)

Calories: 24
Carbohydrate: 1 g
Calories From Fat: 26%
Total Fat: 1 g
Saturated Fat: <1 g
Cholesterol: 27 mg
Sodium: 96 mg
Dietary Fiber: 1 g
Protein: 3 g

picante vegetable dip

⅔ cup reduced-fat sour cream
½ cup picante sauce
⅓ cup mayonnaise or reduced-fat mayonnaise
¼ cup finely chopped green or red bell pepper
2 tablespoons finely chopped green onion
¾ teaspoon garlic salt
Assorted fresh vegetable dippers

Combine sour cream, picante sauce, mayonnaise, bell pepper, green onion and garlic salt in medium bowl until well blended. Cover; refrigerate several hours or overnight to allow flavors to blend. Serve with dippers.

Makes about 1⅔ cups

nutrients per serving:

2 tablespoons

Calories: 61
Carbohydrate: 2 g
Calories From Fat: 83%
Total Fat: 6 g
Saturated Fat: 2 g
Cholesterol: 8 mg
Sodium: 173 mg
Dietary Fiber: <1 g
Protein: 1 g

angelic deviled eggs

taco popcorn olé

9 cups air-popped popcorn
   Butter-flavored cooking spray
1 teaspoon chili powder
½ teaspoon salt
½ teaspoon garlic powder
⅛ teaspoon ground red pepper (optional)

1. Preheat oven to 350°F. Line 15×10-inch jelly-roll pan with foil.

2. Place popcorn in single layer in prepared pan. Coat lightly with cooking spray.

3. Combine chili powder, salt, garlic powder and red pepper, if desired, in small bowl; sprinkle over popcorn. Mix lightly to coat evenly.

4. Bake 5 minutes or until hot, stirring gently after 3 minutes. Spread mixture in single layer on large sheet of foil to cool.   *Makes 6 (1½-cup) servings*

Tip: Store popcorn mixture in tightly covered container at room temperature up to 4 days.

cheesy chips

10 wonton wrappers
 2 tablespoons powdered American cheese or grated Parmesan cheese
 2 teaspoons olive oil
⅛ teaspoon garlic powder

1. Preheat oven to 375°F. Spray baking sheet with nonstick cooking spray.

2. Diagonally cut each wonton wrapper in half, forming two triangles. Place in single layer on prepared baking sheet.

3. Combine cheese, oil and garlic powder in small bowl. Sprinkle over wonton triangles.

4. Bake 6 to 8 minutes or until golden brown and crisp. Remove from oven. Cool completely.   *Makes 4 servings*

taco popcorn olé

chilled shrimp in chinese mustard sauce

nutrients per serving:

⅙ of total recipe (with about 2 teaspoons mustard sauce)

Calories: 92
Carbohydrate: 5 g
Calories From Fat: 7%
Total Fat: 1 g
Saturated Fat: <1 g
Cholesterol: 116 mg
Sodium: 365 mg
Dietary Fiber: <1 g
Protein: 13 g

1 cup water
½ cup dry white wine
2 tablespoons reduced-sodium soy sauce
½ teaspoon Szechuan or black peppercorns
1 pound raw large shrimp, peeled and deveined
¼ cup prepared sweet and sour sauce
2 teaspoons hot Chinese mustard

1. Combine water, wine, soy sauce and peppercorns in medium saucepan. Bring to a boil over high heat. Add shrimp; reduce heat to medium. Cover and simmer 2 to 3 minutes or until shrimp are opaque. Drain well. Cover and refrigerate until chilled.

2. Combine sweet and sour sauce and mustard in small bowl; mix well. Serve as a dipping sauce for shrimp. *Makes 6 servings*

Health Note: Shellfish, such as shrimp, is an excellent source of low-calorie, low-fat protein. It's also rich in the minerals iron, copper and zinc, yet low in sodium.

grilled turkey ham quesadillas

nutrients per serving:

2 quesadilla quarters (without additional salsa or sour cream)

Calories: 66
Carbohydrate: 8 g
Calories From Fat: 26%
Total Fat: 2 g
Saturated Fat: 1 g
Cholesterol: 5 mg
Sodium: 195 mg
Dietary Fiber: <1 g
Protein: 4 g

Nonstick cooking spray
¼ cup salsa
4 (7-inch) flour tortillas
½ cup (1 ounce) shredded reduced-sodium reduced-fat Monterey Jack cheese
¼ cup finely chopped turkey ham
1 can (4 ounces) diced green chilies, drained
Additional salsa (optional)
Fat-free sour cream (optional)

1. To prevent sticking, spray grid with cooking spray. Prepare coals for grilling.

2. Spread 1 tablespoon salsa onto each tortilla. Sprinkle cheese, turkey ham and chilies equally over half of each tortilla; fold over uncovered half to make "sandwich"; spray tops and bottoms of tortilla "sandwiches" with cooking spray.

3. Grill quesadillas on uncovered grill over medium coals 1½ minutes per side or until cheese is melted and tortillas are golden brown, turning once. Quarter each quesadilla and serve with additional salsa and nonfat sour cream, if desired.

Makes 8 servings

chilled shrimp in chinese mustard sauce

buffalo chicken tenders

nutrients per serving:

about 2 chicken tenders plus 1½ tablespoons dipping sauce

Calories: 83
Carbohydrate: 5 g
Calories From Fat: 27%
Total Fat: 2 g
Saturated Fat: 1 g
Cholesterol: 27 mg
Sodium: 180 mg
Dietary Fiber: 0 g
Protein: 9 g

3 tablespoons Louisiana-style hot sauce
½ teaspoon paprika
¼ teaspoon ground red pepper
1 pound chicken tenders
½ cup fat-free blue cheese dressing
¼ cup reduced-fat sour cream
2 tablespoons crumbled blue cheese
1 medium red bell pepper, cut into ½-inch slices

1. Preheat oven to 375°F. Combine hot sauce, paprika and ground red pepper in small bowl; brush on all surfaces of chicken. Place chicken in greased 11×7-inch baking dish. Cover; marinate in refrigerator 30 minutes.

2. Bake, uncovered, about 15 minutes or until chicken is no longer pink in center.

3. Combine blue cheese dressing, sour cream and blue cheese in small serving bowl. Garnish as desired. Serve with chicken and bell pepper for dipping.

Makes 10 servings

monterey wedges

nutrients per serving:

2 wedges

Calories: 85
Carbohydrate: 8 g
Calories From Fat: 47%
Total Fat: 5 g
Saturated Fat: 1 g
Cholesterol: 5 mg
Sodium: 387 mg
Dietary Fiber: 1 g
Protein: 3 g

2 (6-inch) corn tortillas
¼ cup (1 ounce) shredded reduced-fat Monterey Jack or sharp Cheddar cheese
½ teaspoon chili powder
½ cup chopped green bell pepper
1 plum tomato, chopped (about ¼ cup)
2 tablespoons chopped canned green chilies
¼ cup sliced ripe olives, drained

1. Preheat oven 425°F. Coat nonstick baking sheet with nonstick cooking spray.

2. Place tortillas on baking sheet; top each with 2 tablespoons cheese, half the chili powder, bell pepper, tomato, chilies and olives. Top with remaining 2 tablespoons cheese.

3. Bake 5 minutes or until cheese melts. Remove from oven and let stand on baking sheet 3 minutes for easier handling. Cut into 4 wedges.

Makes 4 servings

buffalo chicken tenders

nutrients per serving:

Calories: 207

Carbohydrate: 3 g

Calories From Fat: 74%

Total Fat: 17 g

Saturated Fat: 10 g

Cholesterol: 48 mg

Sodium: 334 mg

Dietary Fiber: <1 g

Protein: 10 g

easiest three-cheese fondue

1 tablespoon margarine
¼ cup finely chopped onion
2 cloves garlic, minced
1 tablespoon all-purpose flour
¾ cup reduced-fat (2%) milk
2 cups (8 ounces) shredded mild or sharp Cheddar cheese
1 package (3 ounces) cream cheese, cut into cubes
½ cup (2 ounces) crumbled blue cheese
⅛ teaspoon ground red pepper
4 to 6 drops hot pepper sauce
Assorted fresh vegetables for dipping

1. Heat margarine in small saucepan over medium heat until melted. Add onion and garlic; cook and stir 2 to 3 minutes or until tender. Stir in flour; cook 2 minutes, stirring constantly.

2. Stir milk into saucepan; bring to a boil. Boil, stirring constantly, about 1 minute or until thickened. Reduce heat to low; add cheeses, stirring until melted. Stir in red pepper and pepper sauce. Pour fondue into serving dish. Serve with dippers.

Makes 8 (3-tablespoon) servings

Hint: For a special touch, sprinkle fondue with parsley and ground red pepper.

Lighten Up: To reduce the total fat, replace the Cheddar cheese and cream cheese with reduced-fat Cheddar and cream cheeses.

Prep and Cook Time: 20 minutes

easiest three-cheese fondue

nutrients per serving:

2 roll-ups (without garnish)

Calories: 51
Carbohydrate: 4 g
Calories From Fat: 19%
Total Fat: 1 g
Saturated Fat: <1 g
Cholesterol: 10 mg
Sodium: 259 mg
Dietary Fiber: 2 g
Protein: 7 g

turkey-broccoli roll-ups

2 pounds fresh broccoli spears
⅓ cup fat-free sour cream
¼ cup reduced-fat mayonnaise
2 tablespoons thawed frozen orange juice concentrate
1 tablespoon Dijon mustard
1 teaspoon dried basil leaves
1 pound smoked turkey, very thinly sliced

1. Arrange broccoli spears in single layer in large, shallow microwavable dish. Add 1 tablespoon water. Cover dish tightly with plastic wrap; vent. Microwave at HIGH 6 to 7 minutes or just until broccoli is crisp-tender, rearranging spears after 4 minutes. Carefully remove plastic wrap; drain broccoli. Immediately place broccoli in cold water to stop cooking; drain well. Pat dry with paper towels.

2. Combine sour cream, mayonnaise, juice concentrate, mustard and basil in small bowl; mix well.

3. Cut turkey slices into 2-inch-wide strips. Spread sour cream mixture evenly on strips. Place 1 broccoli piece at short end of each strip. Starting at short end, roll up tightly (allow broccoli spear to protrude from one end). Place on serving platter; cover with plastic wrap. Refrigerate until ready to serve. Garnish just before serving, if desired. *Makes 20 servings*

Note: To blanch broccoli on stove top, bring small amount of water to a boil in saucepan. Add broccoli spears; cover. Simmer 2 to 3 minutes or until broccoli is crisp-tender; drain. Cool; continue as directed.

turkey-broccoli roll-ups

nutrients per serving:

4 pieces

Calories: 56
Carbohydrate: 8 g
Calories From Fat: 29%
Total Fat: 2 g
Saturated Fat: <1 g
Cholesterol: 0 mg
Sodium: 187 mg
Dietary Fiber: 2 g
Protein: 3 g

hummus-stuffed vegetables

1 can (15 ounces) chick-peas, rinsed and drained
1 medium clove garlic
1 tablespoon lemon juice
1 tablespoon olive oil
½ teaspoon ground cumin
¼ teaspoon salt
¼ teaspoon black pepper
1 cup Chinese pea pods (about 24)
¾ pound medium fresh mushrooms (about 24)

1. Combine chick-peas, garlic, lemon juice, oil, cumin, salt and pepper in food processor. Process until smooth. Transfer to piping bag fitted with fluted tip.

2. Remove strings from pea pods. Carefully split pea pods with tip of paring knife. Remove stems from mushrooms; discard.

3. Pipe bean mixture into pea pods and into cavities of inverted mushrooms. Store loosely covered in refrigerator until ready to serve. Garnish just before serving, if desired. *Makes 12 servings*

Variation: Substitute cucumber slices or red or green bell peppers, cut into 1½-inch triangles, for pea pods and mushrooms.

hummus-stuffed vegetables

swimming tuna dip

1 cup low-fat (1%) cottage cheese
1 tablespoon reduced-fat mayonnaise
1 tablespoon lemon juice
2 teaspoons dry ranch-style salad dressing mix
1 can (3 ounces) chunk white tuna packed in water, drained and
**   flaked**
2 tablespoons sliced green onion or chopped celery
1 teaspoon dried parsley flakes
1 package (12 ounces) peeled baby carrots

Combine cottage cheese, mayonnaise, lemon juice and salad dressing mix in food processor or blender. Cover and blend until smooth. Stir in tuna, green onion and parsley. Serve with carrots.   *Makes 4 servings*

curly lettuce wrappers

4 green leaf lettuce leaves
¼ cup reduced-fat sour cream
4 turkey bacon slices, crisp-cooked and crumbled
½ cup (2 ounces) crumbled feta or blue cheese
8 ounces thinly sliced deli turkey breast
4 whole green onions
½ medium red or green bell pepper, thinly sliced
1 cup broccoli sprouts

1. Rinse lettuce leaves and pat dry.

2. Combine sour cream and bacon in small bowl. Spread ¼ of sour cream mixture evenly over center third of one lettuce leaf. Sprinkle 2 tablespoons cheese over sour cream. Top with 2 ounces turkey.

3. Cut off green portion of each green onion, reserving white onion bottoms for later use. Place green portion of 1 onion, ¼ of bell pepper slices and ¼ cup sprouts on top of turkey.

4. Fold right edge of lettuce over filling; fold bottom edge up over filling. Loosely roll up from folded right edge, leaving left edge of wrap open. Repeat with remaining ingredients.   *Makes 4 servings*

swimming tuna dip

mini marinated beef skewers

nutrients per serving:

3 skewers (without cherry tomatoes and lettuce)

Calories: 120
Carbohydrate: 2 g
Calories From Fat: 30%
Total Fat: 4 g
Saturated Fat: 1 g
Cholesterol: 60 mg
Sodium: 99 mg
Dietary Fiber: <1 g
Protein: 20 g

1 beef top round steak (about 1 pound)
2 tablespoons reduced-sodium soy sauce
1 tablespoon dry sherry
1 teaspoon dark sesame oil
2 cloves garlic, minced
18 cherry tomatoes (optional)

1. Cut beef crosswise into ⅛-inch slices. Place in large resealable plastic food storage bag. Combine soy sauce, sherry, oil and garlic in cup; pour over steak. Seal bag; turn to coat. Marinate in refrigerator at least 30 minutes or up to 2 hours.

2. Soak 18 (6-inch) skewers in water 20 minutes.

3. Drain steak; discard marinade. Weave beef accordion-style onto skewers. Place on rack of broiler pan.

4. Broil 4 to 5 inches from heat 2 minutes. Turn skewers over; broil 2 minutes or until beef is barely pink.

5. If desired, garnish each skewer with 1 cherry tomato. Place skewers on lettuce-lined platter. Serve warm.   *Makes 6 servings (3 skewers each)*

mini marinated beef skewers

ham and cheese "sushi" rolls

nutrients per serving:

8 pieces

Calories: 145
Carbohydrate: 3 g
Calories From Fat: 81%
Total Fat: 13 g
Saturated Fat: 12 g
Cholesterol: 40 mg
Sodium: 263 mg
Dietary Fiber: <1 g
Protein: 5 g

4 thin slices deli ham (about 4×4 inches)
1 package (8 ounces) cream cheese, softened
1 seedless cucumber, quartered lengthwise and cut into 4-inch
**   lengths**
4 thin slices (about 4×4 inches) American or Cheddar cheese,
**   at room temperature**
1 red bell pepper, cut into thin 4-inch-long strips

1. For ham sushi: Pat each ham slice with paper towel to remove excess moisture. Spread each ham slice to edges with 2 tablespoons cream cheese.

2. Pat 1 cucumber quarter with paper towel to remove excess moisture; place at edge of ham slice. Roll tightly. Seal by pressing gently. Roll in plastic wrap; refrigerate. Repeat with remaining three ham slices.

3. For cheese sushi: Spread each cheese slice to edges with 2 tablespoons cream cheese.

4. Place 2 strips red pepper even with one edge of one cheese slice. Roll tightly. Seal by pressing gently. Roll in plastic wrap; refrigerate. Repeat with remaining 3 cheese slices.

5. To serve: Remove plastic wrap from ham and cheese rolls. Cut each roll into 8 (½-inch-wide) pieces. Arrange on platter.   *Makes 8 servings*

ham and cheese "sushi" rolls

best of the wurst spread

nutrients per serving:

Calories: 168
Carbohydrate: 2 g
Calories From Fat: 86%
Total Fat: 16 g
Saturated Fat: 5 g
Cholesterol: 64 mg
Sodium: 128 mg
Dietary Fiber: <1 g
Protein: 5 g

1 tablespoon butter or margarine
½ cup finely chopped onion
1 package (16 ounces) liverwurst
¼ cup mayonnaise or salad dressing
¼ cup finely chopped dill pickle
2 teaspoons horseradish mustard or spicy brown mustard
1 tablespoon drained capers
2 teaspoons dried dill weed
¼ small dill pickle, cut into strips
Cocktail rye bread for serving

1. Heat butter in small saucepan over medium heat until melted. Add onion; cook and stir 5 minutes or until tender. Mash liverwurst with fork in medium bowl; beat in onion, mayonnaise, chopped dill pickle, mustard, capers and dill weed.

2. Form liverwurst mixture into football shape on serving plate; decorate with dill pickle strips to look like football laces. Serve with bread.

Makes 12 (3-tablespoon) servings

Serving Suggestion: For added flavor, serve the spread with mustard toast instead of rye bread. To prepare mustard toast, lightly spread horseradish mustard or spicy brown mustard on cocktail rye bread slices. Broil, 4 inches from heat, until lightly browned.

Prep and Cook Time: 15 minutes

mini burgers

1 pound ground chicken
¼ cup Italian-style dry bread crumbs
¼ cup chili sauce
1 egg white
1 tablespoon white Worcestershire sauce
2 teaspoons Dijon-style mustard
½ teaspoon dried thyme leaves
¼ teaspoon garlic powder
32 thin slices plum tomatoes (about 3 medium)
½ cup sweet onion slices (about 1 small)
16 slices cocktail rye or pumpernickel bread
Mustard (optional)
Pickle slices (optional)
Snipped chives or green onion tops (optional)

1. Preheat oven to 350°F. Combine chicken, bread crumbs, chili sauce, egg white, Worcestershire sauce, mustard, thyme and garlic powder in medium bowl. Form mixture into 16 patties.

2. Place patties in 15×10-inch jelly-roll pan. Bake, uncovered, 10 to 15 minutes or until patties are no longer pink in centers.

3. Place 2 tomato slices and 1 onion slice on each bread slice. Top each with 1 patty; add dollops of mustard, pickle slices and chives, if desired.

Makes 16 servings

nutrients per serving:

1 burger

Calories: 74
Carbohydrate: 7 g
Calories From Fat: 27%
Total Fat: 2 g
Saturated Fat: 1 g
Cholesterol: 14 mg
Sodium: 149 mg
Dietary Fiber: 1 g
Protein: 6 g

dazzling desserts

chocolate peanut butter ice cream sandwiches

nutrients per serving:

1 cookie

Calories: 129
Carbohydrate: 15 g
Calories From Fat: 49%
Total Fat: 7 g
Saturated Fat: 3 g
Cholesterol: 4 mg
Sodium: 124 mg
Dietary Fiber: 1 g
Protein: 4 g

2 tablespoons creamy peanut butter
8 chocolate wafer cookies
⅔ cup no-sugar-added vanilla ice cream, softened

1. Spread peanut butter over flat sides of all cookies.

2. Spoon ice cream over peanut butter on 4 cookies. Top with remaining 4 cookies, peanut butter sides down. Press down lightly to force ice cream to edges of sandwich.

3. Wrap each sandwich in foil; seal tightly. Freeze at least 2 hours or up to 5 days.

Makes 4 servings

café au lait ice cream sundae

nutrients per serving:

Calories: 798
Carbohydrate: 12 g
Calories From Fat: 92%
Total Fat: 82 g
Saturated Fat: 44 g
Cholesterol: 459 mg
Sodium: 79 mg
Dietary Fiber: 1 g
Protein: 9 g

3 cups whipping cream, divided
4 egg yolks, lightly beaten
1 tablespoon instant coffee granules
½ cup plus 2 tablespoons no-calorie sugar substitute for baking, divided
½ teaspoon vanilla
½ cup chopped walnuts or pecans

1. Pour 2 cups cream into medium saucepan. Whisk egg yolks and coffee granules into cream. Heat 10 minutes over low heat, stirring constantly, until mixture reaches 160°F. Mixture will thicken as it cooks.

2. Pour mixture into bowl, stir in ½ cup sugar substitute until well blended. Refrigerate 2 to 3 hours or until cold. Pour chilled mixture into ice cream maker; process according to manufacturer's directions.

3. Whip remaining 1 cup cream, 2 tablespoons sugar substitute and vanilla until stiff. Scoop ice cream into serving bowls; top with whipped cream. Sprinkle with nuts just before serving.

Makes 4 servings

chocolate peanut butter ice cream sandwiches

nutrients per serving:

Calories: 205
Carbohydrate: 15 g
Calories From Fat: 66%
Total Fat: 15 g
Saturated Fat: 9 g
Cholesterol: 36 mg
Sodium: 127 mg
Dietary Fiber: <1 g
Protein: 3 g

strawberry-topped cheesecake cups

1 cup sliced strawberries
10 packages sugar substitute, divided
1 teaspoon vanilla, divided
½ teaspoon grated orange peel
¼ teaspoon grated fresh ginger
1 package (8 ounces) cream cheese, softened
½ cup sour cream
2 tablespoons granulated sugar
16 vanilla wafers, crushed

1. Combine strawberries, 1 package sugar substitute, ¼ teaspoon vanilla, orange peel and grated ginger in medium bowl; toss gently. Let stand 20 minutes to allow flavors to blend.

2. Meanwhile, combine cream cheese, sour cream, remaining 9 packets sugar substitute and granulated sugar in medium mixing bowl. Add remaining ¾ teaspoon vanilla; beat 30 seconds on low speed of electric mixer. Increase to medium speed; beat 30 seconds or until smooth.

3. Spoon cream cheese mixture into 8 individual ¼-cup ramekins. Top each with about 2 tablespoons vanilla wafer crumbs and about 2 tablespoons strawberry mixture.

Makes 8 servings

nutrients per serving:

½ cup

Calories: 193
Carbohydrate: 15 g
Calories From Fat: 68%
Total Fat: 15 g
Saturated Fat: 9 g
Cholesterol: 54 mg
Sodium: 15 mg
Dietary Fiber: 3 g
Protein: 2 g

easy raspberry ice cream

8 ounces (1¾ cups) frozen unsweetened raspberries (not frozen in syrup or juice)
2 to 3 tablespoons powdered sugar
½ cup whipping cream

In food processor fitted with steel blade, process raspberries 15 minutes using on/off pulsing action or until they resemble coarse crumbs. Add sugar and process about 5 seconds or until thoroughly blended. With machine running, slowly add cream and process about 10 seconds or until well combined and raspberries have lightened in color. Serve immediately.

Makes 3 servings

strawberry-topped cheesecake cups

speedy pineapple-lime sorbet

nutrients per serving:

½ cup sorbet

Calories: 56
Carbohydrate: 15 g
Calories From Fat: 5%
Total Fat: <1 g
Saturated Fat: <1 g
Cholesterol: 0 mg
Sodium: 1 mg
Dietary Fiber: 1 g
Protein: <1 g

1 ripe pineapple, cut into cubes (about 4 cups)
⅓ cup frozen limeade concentrate, thawed
1 to 2 tablespoons fresh lime juice
1 teaspoon grated lime peel

1. Arrange pineapple in single layer on large baking sheet; freeze at least 1 hour or until very firm. Use metal spatula to transfer pineapple to resealable plastic freezer food storage bags; freeze up to 1 month.

2. Combine frozen pineapple, limeade, lime juice and lime peel in food processor; process until smooth and fluffy. If pineapple doesn't become smooth and fluffy, let stand 30 minutes to soften slightly; then repeat processing. Serve immediately.

Makes 8 servings

Note: This dessert is best if served immediately; but it may be made ahead, stored in the freezer, then softened several minutes before being served.

cherry-peach pops

nutrients per serving:

1 pop

Calories: 52
Carbohydrate: 11 g
Calories From Fat: 1%
Total Fat: <1 g
Saturated Fat: <1 g
Cholesterol: 1 mg
Sodium: 34 mg
Dietary Fiber: <1 g
Protein: 2 g

⅓ cup peach nectar or apricot nectar
1 teaspoon unflavored gelatin
1 (15-ounce) can sliced peaches in light syrup, drained
1 (6- or 8-ounce) carton fat-free sugar-free peach or cherry yogurt
1 (6- or 8-ounce) carton fat-free sugar-free cherry yogurt

1. Combine nectar and unflavored gelatin in small saucepan; let stand 5 minutes. Heat and stir over low heat just until gelatin dissolves.

2. Combine nectar mixture, drained peaches and yogurts in food processor. Cover and process until smooth.

3. Pour into 7 (3-ounce) paper cups, filling each about ⅔ full. Place in freezer; freeze 1 hour. Insert wooden stick into center of each cup. Freeze at least 3 more hours.

4. Let stand at room temperature 10 minutes before serving. Tear away paper cups to serve.

Makes 7 servings

speedy pineapple-lime sorbet

nutrients per serving:

1 bar

Calories: 105
Carbohydrate: 11 g
Calories From Fat: 60%
Total Fat: 7 g
Saturated Fat: 3 g
Cholesterol: 22 mg
Sodium: 54 mg
Dietary Fiber: <1 g
Protein: 1 g

currant cheesecake bars

½ cup (1 stick) butter, softened
1 cup all-purpose flour
½ cup packed light brown sugar
½ cup finely chopped pecans
1 package (8 ounces) cream cheese, softened
¼ cup granulated sugar
1 egg
1 tablespoon milk
2 teaspoons grated lemon peel
⅓ cup currant jelly or seedless raspberry jam

1. Preheat oven to 350°F. Grease 9-inch square baking pan. Beat butter in medium bowl with electric mixer at medium speed until smooth. Add flour, brown sugar and pecans; beat at low speed until well blended. Press mixture into bottom and partially up sides of prepared pan.

2. Bake about 15 minutes or until light brown. If sides of crust have slumped down, press back up and reshape with spoon. Let cool 5 minutes on wire rack.

3. Meanwhile, beat cream cheese in large bowl with electric mixer at medium speed until smooth. Add granulated sugar, egg, milk and lemon peel; beat until well blended.

4. Heat jelly in small saucepan over low heat 2 to 3 minutes or until smooth, stirring occasionally.

5. Pour cream cheese mixture over crust. Drizzle jelly in 7 to 8 horizontal strips across filling with spoon. Swirl jelly through filling with knife to create marbled effect.

6. Bake 20 to 25 minutes or until filling is set. Cool completely on wire rack before cutting into bars. Store in airtight container in refrigerator up to 1 week.

Makes about 32 bars

currant cheesecake bars

chocolate-caramel s'mores

nutrients per serving:

1 s'more

Calories: 72
Carbohydrate: 14 g
Calories From Fat: 23%
Total Fat: 2 g
Saturated Fat: 1 g
Cholesterol: 0 mg
Sodium: 77 mg
Dietary Fiber: 0 g
Protein: 1 g

12 chocolate wafer cookies or chocolate graham cracker squares
2 tablespoons fat-free caramel topping
6 large marshmallows

1. Prepare coals for grilling. Place 6 wafer cookies top down on plate. Spread 1 teaspoon caramel topping in center of each wafer to within about ¼ inch of edge.

2. Spear 1 to 2 marshmallows onto long wood-handled skewer.* Hold several inches above coals 3 to 5 minutes or until marshmallows are golden and very soft, turning slowly. Push 1 marshmallow off into center of caramel. Top with plain wafer. Repeat with remaining marshmallows and wafers. *Makes 6 servings*

*If wood-handled skewers are unavailable, use oven mitt to protect hand from heat.

Note: S'mores, a favorite campfire treat, got their name because everyone who tasted them wanted "some more." In the unlikely event of leftover S'Mores, they can be reheated in the microwave at HIGH 15 to 30 seconds.

frozen berry ice cream

nutrients per serving:

½ cup

Calories: 69
Carbohydrate: 15 g
Calories From Fat: 2%
Total Fat: <1 g
Saturated Fat: <1 g
Cholesterol: 0 mg
Sodium: 23 mg
Dietary Fiber: 1 g
Protein: 3 g

8 ounces frozen unsweetened strawberries, partially thawed
8 ounces frozen unsweetened peaches, partially thawed
4 ounces frozen unsweetened blueberries, partially thawed
6 packets sugar substitute
2 teaspoons vanilla
2 cups no-sugar-added light vanilla ice cream
16 blueberries
4 small strawberries, halved
8 peach slices

1. Combine frozen strawberries, peaches, blueberries, sugar substitute and vanilla in food processor. Process until coarsely chopped.

2. Add ice cream; process until well blended.

3. Serve immediately for semi-soft texture or freeze until needed and allow to stand 10 minutes to soften slightly. Garnish each serving with 2 blueberries, 1 strawberry half and 1 peach slice. *Makes 8 servings*

chocolate-caramel s'mores

nutrients per serving:

Calories: 147
Carbohydrate: 12 g
Calories From Fat: 56%
Total Fat: 9 g
Saturated Fat: 6 g
Cholesterol: 34 mg
Sodium: 111 mg
Dietary Fiber: <1 g
Protein: 4 g

pineapple-ginger bavarian

1 can (8 ounces) crushed pineapple in juice, drained and liquid reserved
1 package (4 serving size) sugar-free orange gelatin
1 cup sugar-free ginger ale
1 cup plain nonfat yogurt
¾ teaspoon grated fresh ginger
½ cup whipping cream
1 packet sugar substitute
¼ teaspoon vanilla

1. Combine reserved pineapple juice with enough water to equal ½ cup liquid. Pour into small saucepan. Bring to a boil over high heat.

2. Place gelatin in medium bowl. Add pineapple juice mixture; stir until gelatin is completely dissolved. Add ginger ale and half of crushed pineapple; stir until well blended. Add yogurt; whisk until well blended. Pour into 5 individual ramekins. Cover each ramekin with plastic wrap; refrigerate until firm.

3. Meanwhile, combine remaining half of pineapple with ginger in small bowl. Cover with plastic wrap; refrigerate.

4. Just before serving, beat cream in small deep bowl at high speed of electric mixer until soft peaks form. Add sugar substitute and vanilla; beat until stiff peaks form.

5. To serve, top each bavarian with 1 tablespoon whipped topping and 1 tablespoon pineapple mixture.   *Makes 5 servings*

Tip: Use 2 tablespoons ready-made whipped topping to garnish, if desired.

pineapple-ginger bavarian

nutrients per serving:

Calories: 82
Carbohydrate: 15 g
Calories From Fat: 14%
Total Fat: 1 g
Saturated Fat: <1 g
Cholesterol: 0 mg
Sodium: 25 mg
Dietary Fiber: 2 g
Protein: 3 g

strawberry bavarian deluxe

½ **bag whole frozen unsweetened strawberries (1 mounded quart), partially thawed**
¼ **cup low-sugar strawberry preserves**
¼ **cup granular sucralose**
2 **tablespoons balsamic vinegar**
¾ **cup water, divided**
2 **envelopes (7g each) unflavored gelatin**
1 **tablespoon honey**
½ **cup pasteurized liquid egg whites or 4 egg whites***
½ **teaspoon cream of tartar**
1 **teaspoon vanilla**
1 **pint strawberries, washed, dried and hulled**
1 **cup thawed frozen light whipped topping**
 Mint sprigs (optional)

Use only clean, uncracked eggs.

1. Place strawberries, preserves and sucralose in food processor fitted with steel blade. Process until smooth. Transfer mixture to bowl. Set aside.

2. Combine vinegar with ¼ cup water in small saucepan. Sprinkle in gelatin and let stand until softened. Stir in remaining ½ cup water and honey. Cook and stir over medium heat until gelatin dissolves.

3. Whisk gelatin mixture into berry mixture in bowl. Refrigerate, covered, until mixture is soupy, but not set.

4. Meanwhile, combine liquid egg whites and cream of tartar in bowl. When berry-gelatin mixture is soupy, whip egg whites until soft peaks form.

5. Gently fold egg whites, ⅓ at a time, into chilled berry mixture until mixture is uniform in color. Pour mousse into prechilled 2-quart mold, such as nonstick bundt pan. Refrigerate covered for at least 8 hours or overnight.

6. To serve, run tip of knife around top of mold. Dip mold briefly into large bowl of hot water to loosen. To unmold, center flat serving plate on top of mold, hold firmly so mold doesn't shift, and invert plate and mold. Shake gently to release. Remove mold and refrigerate 10 to 15 minutes. Garnish with fresh strawberries and mint sprigs, if desired. Cut into wedges and serve with 2 tablespoons whipped topping.

Makes 10 servings

strawberry bavarian deluxe

nutrients per serving:

1 square (⅑ of total recipe)

Calories: 98
Carbohydrate: 11 g
Calories From Fat: 24%
Total Fat: 3 g
Saturated Fat: 2 g
Cholesterol: 8 mg
Sodium: 223 mg
Dietary Fiber: 1 g
Protein: 7 g

streusel-topped strawberry cheesecake squares

1 container (8 ounces) strawberry-flavored nonfat yogurt with aspartame sweetener
1 package (8 ounces) fat-free cream cheese
4 ounces reduced-fat cream cheese
6 packets sugar substitute *or* equivalent of ¼ cup sugar
1 packet unflavored gelatin
2 tablespoons water
1 cup fresh chopped strawberries
1 tablespoon sugar
1 cup fresh sliced strawberries
⅓ cup low-fat granola

1. Line 9-inch square baking pan with plastic wrap, leaving 4-inch overhang on 2 opposite sides.

2. Combine yogurt, cream cheese and sugar substitute in medium bowl; beat until smooth. Set aside.

3. Combine gelatin and water in small microwavable bowl; let stand 2 minutes. Microwave at HIGH 40 seconds to dissolve gelatin. Beat gelatin into yogurt mixture. Combine chopped strawberries and sugar in small bowl. Add to yogurt mixture.

4. Pour yogurt mixture evenly into prepared pan. Refrigerate 1 hour or until firm.

5. Just before serving, arrange 1 cup sliced strawberries on top; sprinkle with granola.

6. Gently lift cheesecake out of pan with plastic wrap. Pull plastic wrap away from sides; cut into 9 to 12 squares. *Makes 9 to 12 servings*

recipe index

A

Angelic Deviled Eggs, 212

Apple and Brie Omelet, 110

Asian Chicken Kabobs, 176

Asparagus
Oven-Roasted Asparagus, 193
Stir-Fried Asparagus, 200

Autumn Casserole, 196

Avocado
Grilled Red Snapper with Avocado-Papaya Salsa, 132
Pan Seared Halibut Steaks with Avocado Salsa, 146

B

Bacon
Bacon & Cheese Dip, 208
Curly Lettuce Wrappers, 226

Bacon & Cheese Dip, 208

Baked Eggs, 106

Baked Eggs Florentine, 114

Balsamic Vinaigrette, 200

Beans: Hummus-Stuffed Vegetables, 224

Beef
Blue Cheese-Stuffed Sirloin Patties, 158
Braciola, 173

Beef (continued)
Flank Steak with Italian Salsa, 138
Mini Marinated Beef Skewers, 228
Pasta Meatball Soup, 148
Peppercorn Steaks, 122
Seared Beef Tenderloin with Horseradish-Rosemary Cream, 120
Sirloin with Sweet Caramelized Onions, 154
Steaks with Zesty Merlot Sauce, 128
Stir-Fry Beef & Vegetable Soup, 164

Berries
Currant Cheesecake Bars, 240
Easy Raspberry Ice Cream, 236
Frozen Berry Ice Cream, 242
Red and Greens Salad, 190
Strawberry Bavarian Deluxe, 246
Strawberry Blueberry Salsa, 188
Strawberry-Topped Cheesecake Cups, 236
Streusel-Topped Strawberry Cheesecake Squares, 248

Best of the Wurst Spread, 232

Blackened Chicken Salad, 152

Blue Cheese-Stuffed Sirloin Patties, 158

Braciola, 173

Broccoli
Broccoli Italian Style, 193
Broccoli with Creamy Lemon Sauce, 202
Chicken and Vegetable Chowder, 182
Easy Brunch Frittata, 118
Ham & Cheddar Frittata, 106
Turkey-Broccoli Roll-Ups, 222

Broccoli Italian Style, 193

Broccoli with Creamy Lemon Sauce, 202

Brunch Eggs Olé, 108

Buffalo Chicken Tenders, 218

Buttermilk-Herb Dressing, 196

C

Café au Lait Ice Cream Sundae, 234

Cauliflower
Indian-Style Vegetable Stir-Fry, 204
Pork Curry over Cauliflower Couscous, 168

Cheesy Chips, 214

Cherry-Peach Pops, 238

Chicken & Turkey
Asian Chicken Kabobs, 176
Blackened Chicken Salad, 152
Buffalo Chicken Tenders, 218
Chicken and Vegetable Chowder, 182
Chicken Teriyaki, 174
Chunky Chicken and Vegetable Soup, 122
Curly Lettuce Wrappers, 226
Curried Chicken & Zucchini Salad, 150
Easy Chicken Salad, 146
Grilled Chicken with Chimichurri Salsa, 160
Grilled Turkey Ham Quesadillas, 216
Jalapeño-Lime Chicken, 126
Jerk Wings with Ranch Dipping Sauce, 206
Main Dish Chicken Soup, 140
Mexican Tortilla Soup, 184
Mini Burgers, 233
Roasted Rosemary Chicken Legs, 150
Roast Turkey Breast with Spinach-Blue Cheese Stuffing, 134

Chicken & Turkey
(continued)
Spinach, Cheese and Prosciutto-Stuffed Chicken Breasts, 162
Thai Noodle Soup, 130
Turkey-Broccoli Roll-Ups, 222
Wild Wedges, 208
Chicken and Vegetable Chowder, 182
Chicken Teriyaki, 174
Chile Cheese Puff, 116
Chilled Shrimp in Chinese Mustard Sauce, 216

Chocolate
Chocolate-Caramel S'Mores, 242
Chocolate Peanut Butter Ice Cream Sandwiches, 234
Chocolate-Caramel S'Mores, 242
Chocolate Peanut Butter Ice Cream Sandwiches, 234
Chunky Chicken and Vegetable Soup, 122
Crustless Southern Quiche, 170
Curly Lettuce Wrappers, 226
Currant Cheesecake Bars, 240

Curried Chicken & Zucchini Salad, 150

D
Deep South Ham and Redeye Gravy, 118

Dips & Spreads
Bacon & Cheese Dip, 208
Best of the Wurst Spread, 232
Easiest Three-Cheese Fondue, 220
Peaches and Creamy Dip with Waffle Wedges, 210
Picante Vegetable Dip, 212
Roasted Garlic Spread with Three Cheeses, 210
Swimming Tuna Dip, 226

Dressings & Sauces
Balsamic Vinaigrette, 200
Buttermilk-Herb Dressing, 196
Fresh Salsa, 109
Ranch Salad Dressing, 154
Stilton Salad Dressing, 194
Strawberry Blueberry Salsa, 188

E
Easiest Three-Cheese Fondue, 220

Easy Brunch Frittata, 118
Easy Chicken Salad, 146
Easy Raspberry Ice Cream, 236

Egg Dishes
Angelic Deviled Eggs, 212
Apple and Brie Omelet, 110
Baked Eggs, 106
Baked Eggs Florentine, 114
Brunch Eggs Olé, 108
Chile Cheese Puff, 116
Crustless Southern Quiche, 170
Easy Brunch Frittata, 118
Fabulous Feta Frittata, 144
Greek Isles Omelet, 112
Ham & Cheddar Frittata, 106
Three-Egg Omelet, 116

F
Fabulous Feta Frittata, 144

Fish
Greek-Style Salmon, 180
Grilled Red Snapper with Avocado-Papaya Salsa, 132

Fish *(continued)*
Grilled Tilapia with Zesty Mustard Sauce, 156
Lime-Poached Fish with Corn and Chili Salsa, 178
Pan Seared Halibut Steaks with Avocado Salsa, 146
Swimming Tuna Dip, 226
Vermouth Salmon, 160
Flank Steak with Italian Salsa, 138
Fresh Salsa, 109
Frozen Berry Ice Cream, 242

G
Greek Isles Omelet, 112
Greek-Style Salmon, 180
Grilled Chicken with Chimichurri Salsa, 160
Grilled Red Snapper with Avocado-Papaya Salsa, 132
Grilled Tilapia with Zesty Mustard Sauce, 156
Grilled Turkey Ham Quesadillas, 216
Grilled Vegetables, 194

H
Ham
Baked Eggs Florentine, 114

Ham *(continued)*
Deep South Ham and Redeye Gravy, 118
Grilled Turkey Ham Quesadillas, 216
Ham & Cheddar Frittata, 106
Ham and Cheese "Sushi" Rolls, 230
Spinach, Cheese and Prosciutto-Stuffed Chicken Breasts, 162
Three-Egg Omelet, 116
Ham & Cheddar Frittata, 106
Ham and Cheese "Sushi" Rolls, 230
Hummus-Stuffed Vegetables, 224

I
Indian-Style Vegetable Stir-Fry, 204

J
Jalapeño-Lime Chicken, 126
Jalapeño Wild Rice Cakes, 186
Jerk Wings with Ranch Dipping Sauce, 206

L
Lemony Cabbage Slaw with Curry, 188

Lime-Poached Fish with Corn and Chili Salsa, 178

M
Main Dish Chicken Soup, 140
Maple-Mustard Pork Chops, 128
Marinated Tomato Salad, 198
Mediterranean Shrimp Soup, 166
Mexican Tortilla Soup, 184
Mini Burgers, 233
Mini Marinated Beef Skewers, 228
Monterey Wedges, 218
Mushrooms
Asian Chicken Kabobs, 176
Autumn Casserole, 196
Chicken and Vegetable Chowder, 182
Hummus-Stuffed Vegetables, 224
Mediterranean Shrimp Soup, 166
Spaghetti Squash Primavera, 136

N
Nuts
Café au Lait Ice Cream Sundae, 234
Currant Cheesecake Bars, 240

Fabulous Feta Frittata, 144

O
Oven-Roasted Asparagus, 193

P
Pan Seared Halibut Steaks with Avocado Salsa, 146
Pasta Meatball Soup, 148
Peaches and Creamy Dip with Waffle Wedges, 210
Peppercorn Steaks, 122
Picante Vegetable Dip, 212
Pineapple-Ginger Bavarian, 244
Pork *(see also* **Bacon; Ham; Sausage**)
Maple-Mustard Pork Chops, 128
Pork Chops Paprikash, 142
Pork Curry over Cauliflower Couscous, 168
Tex-Mex Pork Kabobs with Chili Sour Cream Sauce, 172
Pork Chops Paprikash, 142
Pork Curry over Cauliflower Couscous, 168

R
Ranch Salad Dressing, 154
Red and Greens Salad, 190
Roasted Garlic Spread with Three Cheeses, 210
Roasted Rosemary Chicken Legs, 150
Roast Turkey Breast with Spinach-Blue Cheese Stuffing, 134

S
Salads
Blackened Chicken Salad, 152
Curried Chicken & Zucchini Salad, 150
Easy Chicken Salad, 146
Lemony Cabbage Slaw with Curry, 188
Marinated Tomato Salad, 198
Red and Greens Salad, 190
Tabbouleh, 192
Sausage
Best of the Wurst Spread, 232
Braciola, 173
Crustless Southern Quiche, 170
Seared Beef Tenderloin with Horseradish-Rosemary Cream, 120

Shellfish
Chilled Shrimp in Chinese Mustard Sauce, 216
Mediterranean Shrimp Soup, 166
Szechwan Seafood Stir-Fry, 124
Sirloin with Sweet Caramelized Onions, 154

Slow Cooker Recipes
Bacon & Cheese Dip, 208
Braciola, 173
Chicken and Vegetable Chowder, 182
Mediterranean Shrimp Soup, 166

Soups & Chowders
Chicken and Vegetable Chowder, 182
Chunky Chicken and Vegetable Soup, 122
Main Dish Chicken Soup, 140
Mediterranean Shrimp Soup, 166
Mexican Tortilla Soup, 184
Pasta Meatball Soup, 148
Stir-Fry Beef & Vegetable Soup, 164
Thai Noodle Soup, 130
Spaghetti Squash Primavera, 136
Speedy Pineapple-Lime Sorbet, 238

Spinach
Autumn Casserole, 196
Baked Eggs Florentine, 114
Blackened Chicken Salad, 152
Crustless Southern Quiche, 170
Greek Isles Omelet, 112
Roast Turkey Breast with Spinach-Blue Cheese Stuffing, 134
Spinach, Cheese and Prosciutto-Stuffed Chicken Breasts, 162
Szechwan Seafood Stir-Fry, 124
Spinach, Cheese and Prosciutto-Stuffed Chicken Breasts, 162
Steaks with Zesty Merlot Sauce, 128
Stilton Salad Dressing, 194
Stir-Fried Asparagus, 200
Stir-Fry Beef & Vegetable Soup, 164
Strawberry Bavarian Deluxe, 246
Strawberry Blueberry Salsa, 188
Strawberry-Topped Cheesecake Cups, 236
Streusel-Topped Strawberry Cheesecake Squares, 248

Sun-Dried Tomato Scones, 190
Swimming Tuna Dip, 226
Szechwan Seafood Stir-Fry, 124

T
Tabbouleh, 192
Taco Popcorn Olé, 214
Tex-Mex Pork Kabobs with Chili Sour Cream Sauce, 172
Thai Noodle Soup, 130
Three-Egg Omelet, 116

Tomatoes, Fresh
Blackened Chicken Salad, 152
Flank Steak with Italian Salsa, 138
Fresh Salsa, 109
Lime-Poached Fish with Corn and Chili Salsa, 178
Marinated Tomato Salad, 198
Mexican Tortilla Soup, 184
Mini Burgers, 233
Monterey Wedges, 218
Pan Seared Halibut Steaks with Avocado Salsa, 146
Spaghetti Squash Primavera, 136
Tabbouleh, 192

Tomatoes, Fresh
(continued)
Vegetable Napoleon, 202
Turkey-Broccoli Roll-Ups, 222

V
Vegetable Napoleon, 202
Vermouth Salmon, 160

W
Wild Wedges, 208

Z
Zucchini
Asian Chicken Kabobs, 176
Blackened Chicken Salad, 152
Curried Chicken & Zucchini Salad, 150
Grilled Vegetables, 194
Spaghetti Squash Primavera, 136
Vegetable Napoleon, 202

general index

A

Addiction, 20, 21
Aerobic exercises, 50–55
Agatston, Arthur, 32
Alcohol, 24, 30, 33, 34
Amino acids, 12
Andrews, Sam S., 24
Antioxidant nutrients, 17, 45
Appetite loss, 16
Arthritis, 30
Atkins, Robert, 22. *See also* The New Atkins for the New You diet.
Atkins' diet, 22–23, 38

B

Bad breath, 10, 16
Balart, Luis A., 24
Beer, 24, 25
Bethea, Morrison C., 24
Blood glucose levels
  and carbohydrates, 8–9
  controlling, 12
  and fat, 12
  and insulin, 8–9, 11, 12
  and protein, 11
Body Mass Index (BMI), 72–73
Bulk. *See* Fiber.

C

Calcium, 17, 19, 44
Calories
  amount consumed, 15
  in Atkins' diet, 23
  burned and exercise intensity, 57
  burned by lean tissue, 15
  burned by walking, 56, 57–58

Calories *(continued)*
  content per food type, 11, 46, 74–103
  diets allowing very few, 16
  in Paleo diet, 27
  per gram carbohydrate, 11, 46
  per gram fat, 11, 46
  per gram protein, 11, 46
  restricting, 30–31
  in Schwarzbein Principle II diet, 30–31
  and weight loss, 46, 48–49
Cancer, 19, 36, 47
Carbohydrate Addict's diet, 20–21, 38
Carbohydrates
  and blood glucose levels, 8–9
  calories per gram, 11, 46
  converted to fat, 10
  critical level in Atkins' diet, 23
  digestion, 8, 36, 68
  and insulin levels, 8–9, 22
  metabolism of, 8–10
  ratio to protein, 15
  types of, 9, 11, 20, 24
Chemical imbalances, 20
Children, 19, 45
Cholesterol, 49
  HDL, 13, 14, 16
  LDL, 19
Constipation, 16
Coradain, Loren, 26

D

Dairy products, 85–87
  and building bones, 17, 45
  fiber and sugar in, 44
  in Paleo diet, 19, 26
Dehydration, 10, 16
Diabetes
  and fat, 28, 30
  and grains, 17
  and high glucose concentration, 12
  and protein consumption, 18
Diets, very low-calorie, 16
Digestion
  of carbohydrates, 8, 36, 68
  and fiber, 46
  of protein, 11, 18
Dizziness, 16
Dropout rates of diet studies, 14

E

Eades, Mary Dan, 28
Eades, Michael R., 28
Exercise
  aerobic, 50–52
  in Atkins' diet, 23
  commitment, 54
  in everyday life, 55
  frequency, 52–53
  health benefits of, 58
  and insulin resistance, 11
  intensity, 53, 54, 56–57
  length, 53–54
  in Paleo diet, 26

Exercise *(continued)*
  in Protein Power LifePlan diet, 28–29
  safety issues, 54, 57, 58–59, 60
  in Schwarzbein Principle II diet, 30
  in South Beach diet, 33
  step aerobics, 61
  strength training, 52–53, 62–67
  and stretching, 57
  and target heart-rate zone, 51, 53, 61
  walking, 56–61
  and weight loss, 43

F

Fasting, 9
Fat
  and blood glucose levels, 12
  burning, 10, 22–23
  calories per gram, 11, 46
  from carbohydrates, 10, 24
  dangers of meals high in, 32
  and diseases, 19
  and exercise intensity, 56–57
  importance of, 11, 46
  and insulin levels, 12, 22, 28, 30
  omega-3, 28
  saturated, 11, 19, 49
  storage and insulin, 12
  trans fat, 28
  types of, 46
  unsaturated, 11

Fatigue, 16
Fiber, 9
    and digestion, 46
    and disease, 19
    and feeling of fullness,
       12, 45, 71
    and glycemic index, 44
    importance of, 46–47
    in Protein Power diet,
       29
Flexibility, 57
Folic acid, 49
Food
    combining types of, 35,
       36–37
    cravings, 32
    diaries, 42–43
    preparation of, 19, 69
    timing of eating, 21,
       37

G
Glucagon, 12
Glucose, 8–9, 11, 12,
    68
Glycemic index (GI),
    68–69
    and fiber, 44
    in Suzanne Somers'
       diet, 34–35
    in Zone diet, 37
Glycogen, 9–10, 12,
    37
Gout, 18
Grains
    and disease, 17, 19
    and fiber, 45

H
HDL. *See* High-density
    lipoprotein.
Health risks of low-carb
    diets, 18, 45

Heart Disease
    and fats, 19, 28
    and fiber, 47
    and folic acid, 49
    and grains, 17
    and low-carb diets,
       14
Heart-rate zone. *See*
    Target heart-rate
    zone.
Heller, Rachael F., 20
Heller, Richard F., 20
Heterocyclic amines
    (HCA), 19
High blood pressure, 18,
    28
High-density lipoprotein
    (HDL), 13, 14
Hormonal balance,
    34–35, 36

I
Injury prevention, 54, 57,
    58–59, 60
Insulin
    and blood glucose
      levels, 8–9, 11, 12
    and carbohydrates,
      8–9, 22
    and fat, 12, 22, 28,
      30
    and glucose, 68
    as medication, 43
    overproduction, 20,
      28, 30, 32
    and protein, 22
Insulin resistance (IR), 11,
    30
Interval training, 60–61

J
Jogging, 61

K
Keating, Peggy
    Norwood, 57
Ketones, 22
Ketosis, 10, 18, 37
Kidneys, 18–19

L
Lactating women, 19
Lactose, 44
LDL. *See* Low-density
    lipoprotein.
Lipolysis, 22
Liver, 9–10, 18, 37
Low-carb diet design,
    42–49
    and dining out, 47
    maintaining proper
      nutrition in, 45–47
    and myths, 48–49
    sample menus, 47–48
    tools, 42–45
Low-density lipoprotein
    (LDL), 14, 19

M
Macronutrient blocks, 37
Medications, 18, 43
Metabolic age, 30
Metabolism
    of carbohydrates,
      8–10
    and disease, 30
    and food cravings, 32
    of insulin, 20, 28, 30,
      32
    malfunction, 22
    and muscles, 52
    reprogramming, 34
Minerals, 47
Multivitamin supplements,
    45

Muscles
    benefits of building,
      62–63
    density of, 63
    frequency of exercising,
      52–53
    glycogen in, 9–10
    and metabolism, 52
    preserving, 15

N
National Cancer Institute,
    19
National Weight Control
    Registry (NWCR),
    14
Nausea, 16
New Atkins for the New
    You, 22–23, 38
New Sugar Busters!,
    24–25, 39
Nibbling, 43
Nutrient values, 74–103
    baked products,
      75–77
    beef products, 77–78
    beverages, 78–80
    cereals, grains, and
      pasta, 80–82
    dairy products, 82–84
    fast foods, 84–87
    fats and oils, 87–88
    finfish and shellfish
      products, 88–89
    fruits and fruit juices,
      89–91
    lamb and veal, 91–92
    legumes and legume
      products, 92–93
    nut and seed products,
      93–94
    pork products, 94–95

Nutrient values
   (continued)
   poultry products,
      95–96
   sausages and luncheon
      meats, 96
   snacks, 96–97
   soups, sauces, and
      gravies, 97–98
   sweets, 98–100
   vegetables and
      vegetable products,
      100–103
Nutrition Facts panel, 43,
   44

O
Obesity, 11
Omega-3 fat, 28
Osteoporosis, 18–19, 45

P
Paleo diet, 26–27, 38
Pancreas, 11, 12, 30
Physical activity. *See*
   Exercise.
Phytochemicals, 19
Phytonutrients, 17, 47
Portion sizes
   importance of, 70–71
   increase in, 43
   in Sugar Busters! diet,
      25
   in Zone diet, 37
Potassium, 19

Pregnancy, 19
Protein
   and blood glucose
      levels, 11
   calories per gram, 11,
      46
   digestion, 11, 18
   importance of, 10–11
   and insulin levels, 22
   and medical conditions,
      18–19
   ratio to carbohydrates,
      15
   Recommended Dietary
      Allowance of, 18
   safe daily amount, 12
Protein Power LifePlan
   diet, 28–29, 38
Pulse, checking, 52

R
Recommended Dietary
   Allowance, 18
Resistance training. *See*
   Strength training.
Reward meals, 20, 21
Roughage. *See* Fiber.

S
Safety, 16–17
Saturated fat, 11, 19, 49
Schwarzbein, Diana, 30
   See also
   Schwarzbein
   Principle II diet.

Schwarzbein Principle II
   diet, 30–31, 39
Sears, Barry, 36
Snacks, 24–25
Somers, Suzanne, 34.
   See also Suzanne
   Somers' diet.
South Beach Diet
   Supercharged,
   32–33, 39
Standard servings, 70–71
Starch, 9
Step aerobics, 61
Steroids, 43
Steward, H. Leighton, 24
Strength training
   benefits of, 52, 62–63
   frequency, 52–53
   guidelines, 63–64
   proper form for, 64
   sample workout, 64–67
Stretching, 57
Stroke, 49
Studies of weight loss,
   13–16, 17
Sugar, 8, 44–45. *See
   also* Glucose.
Sugar Busters! diet,
   24–25, 39
Suzanne Somers' Sexy
   Forever diet, 34–35,
   39

T
Target heart-rate zone,
   51, 53, 61

Trans fat, 28
Triglycerides, 13
U
Unsaturated fat, 11
Urination, 10
U.S. Dietary Guidelines
   for Americans, 15,
   23, 35, 46

V
Very low-calorie diets, 16
Vitamins, 17, 44, 45, 47

W
Walking
   ease of, 51
   interval training, 60–61
   lifestyle, 59–60, 61
   proper form for, 59
   workout, 60
Water, 25
Weight lifting/training.
   See Strength training.
Weight-loss goals, 72–73
Weights, 64
Wilmore, Jack, 57
Wine, 25

Z
Zone diet, 36–37, 39

METRIC CONVERSION CHART

VOLUME MEASUREMENTS (dry)

1/8 teaspoon = 0.5 mL
1/4 teaspoon = 1 mL
1/2 teaspoon = 2 mL
3/4 teaspoon = 4 mL
1 teaspoon = 5 mL
1 tablespoon = 15 mL
2 tablespoons = 30 mL
1/4 cup = 60 mL
1/3 cup = 75 mL
1/2 cup = 125 mL
2/3 cup = 150 mL
3/4 cup = 175 mL
1 cup = 250 mL
2 cups = 1 pint = 500 mL
3 cups = 750 mL
4 cups = 1 quart = 1 L

VOLUME MEASUREMENTS (fluid)

1 fluid ounce (2 tablespoons) = 30 mL
4 fluid ounces (1/2 cup) = 125 mL
8 fluid ounces (1 cup) = 250 mL
12 fluid ounces (1 1/2 cups) = 375 mL
16 fluid ounces (2 cups) = 500 mL

WEIGHTS (mass)

1/2 ounce = 15 g
1 ounce = 30 g
3 ounces = 90 g
4 ounces = 120 g
8 ounces = 225 g
10 ounces = 285 g
12 ounces = 360 g
16 ounces = 1 pound = 450 g

DIMENSIONS

1/16 inch = 2 mm
1/8 inch = 3 mm
1/4 inch = 6 mm
1/2 inch = 1.5 cm
3/4 inch = 2 cm
1 inch = 2.5 cm

OVEN TEMPERATURES

250°F = 120°C
275°F = 140°C
300°F = 150°C
325°F = 160°C
350°F = 180°C
375°F = 190°C
400°F = 200°C
425°F = 220°C
450°F = 230°C

BAKING PAN SIZES

Utensil	Size in Inches/Quarts	Metric Volume	Size in Centimeters
Baking or Cake Pan (square or rectangular)	8×8×2	2 L	20×20×5
	9×9×2	2.5 L	23×23×5
	12×8×2	3 L	30×20×5
	13×9×2	3.5 L	33×23×5
Loaf Pan	8×4×3	1.5 L	20×10×7
	9×5×3	2 L	23×13×7
Round Layer Cake Pan	8×1½	1.2 L	20×4
	9×1½	1.5 L	23×4
Pie Plate	8×1¼	750 mL	20×3
	9×1¼	1 L	23×3
Baking Dish or Casserole	1 quart	1 L	—
	1½ quart	1.5 L	—
	2 quart	2 L	—